)RGE STOUKAS

CW01649137

ANCIENT GREEK WISDOM

by

George Stoukas

Edited by:
Glen Statile
Sam Chekwas

Seaburn Publishing Group
New York

ANCIENT GREEK WISDOM

Seaburn Wisdom is an imprint of Seaburn Publishing Group.

For information write Seaburn Publishers, PO Box 2085, Astoria NY 11102 or visit us online: www.seaburn.com

Library of Congress Cat. Num. in Pub. Data

ISBN: 1-59232-086-4

Adapted by Dr. Sam Chekwas from the original Greek Version titled: Archaios Ellinikos Politismos by George Stoukas
Translated by: Doris Iodannou, Stanley Sarantis, George Bagess
Edited by Professor Glen Statile and Sam Chekwas

The translation of this book was made possible by the support of the following: Thomas Tsogas, Eleni Gioka, Paul & Sophia Nikolos, Thomas Artas, The Society of Epirotes "Anagenesis" Inc., Ladies auxiliary "Souliotissai", Young Epirotans Society, Prophetis Elias Society of Teriahi" Frank & Helen Roussis, and Kleanthis Meimaroglou.

PRINTED IN THE UNITED STATES OF AMERICA

INTRODUCTION

Ancient Greek Wisdom by George Stoukas is the successful result of a concentrated effort to bring to life the thought and achievements of both the better and lesser known of the great intellectual figures of Greek antiquity. Alfred North Whitehead may once have referred to the 17th century as the *Age of Genius*, but the civilization advancing triumphs of those who belong to the pantheon of great Greek thinkers, leaders, and artists of antiquity are second to none in recorded history. If something is only as good or bad as its beginning then we moderns must look back to our beginnings, to the foundation of civilization in Greece, to appreciate our pedigree as joint rulers of a planet that the Greek *cosmologoi* were the first to speculate about in a systematic way.

By making genius in general his focus, a term which only really comes into prominence over the last several centuries, Stoukas is able to avoid the limitations of specialization whereby the compass of his polymathic interests would be caged within the confines of lone topics such as Greek philosophy or Greek drama. The entire Greek world is his stage. Some wise person once defined a specialist as one whose knowledge is a mile deep but only an inch wide, while conversely, the knowledge of the generalist is wide but shallow. Stoukas avoids both extremes, forging a happy marriage which gives birth to a book whose scope will satisfy both the generalist and specialist in each of us. The French philosopher Etienne Gilson, one of the leading exponents of the philosophy of St. Thomas Aquinas in the last century, once said that G.K. Chesterton's book on Aquinas, though written by an amateur, had put all the experts to shame. As a person trained in philosophy I would give the very same tribute to George Stoukas, who is indeed a philosopher in practice if not by profession. We the readers are the beneficiaries of a multi-faceted jewel that shines through on every page. Oscar Wilde once quipped that he lived in terror of not being misunderstood. Only a devotee of Wilde then would not enjoy this wonderfully accessible and understandable book that holds before us the mirror of the past.

Whether you plunge in anywhere or read the book straight through, the result is the same. In either case you will be taken on a tour of the ancient Greek mind, both profound and witty, sublime and savage, capable of the greatest feats of love as well as the worst of treachery. If I may be permitted the transgression of lapsing into Latin in a book about ancient Greece: *Ecce Homo* (Here is man.). From the search for the primary constructive principles of material reality, in which mechanical forces contend with the camouflaged purposes of nature, to the tragic psychology of Aeschylus and other dramatists, in which the balance of nature must always be fully restored, Stoukas guides us through the labyrinth of Greek accomplishment with the assurance of a polished master who takes full responsibility for the education of his apprentices.

This is the dawn of high civilization, when the first stirrings of reason begin to rise to the task of reinterpreting a mythical past into intelligible form. This is the moment when the birth pangs of intellectual maturity begin to beat, and in their pounding transform the heroic labors of Homer and Hercules into theoretical systems that culminate in the rival philosophical visions of Plato and Aristotle. This is the brave new world of which we are all heirs, a time in which both the sacred and the profane often speak with one voice. We are descendants of Prometheus, who by the gift of fire gave to mankind the wherewithal to harness the resources of nature to our own advantage, so that we would not only survive, but flourish.

Thus we all owe a debt of gratitude to George Stoukas for sharing his love of learning with us. Seaburn Press and Sam Chekwas are also to be congratulated for their effort in making this book available to the English speaking community. I look forward to future excellence from the mind and pen of Stoukas, but even he will find it difficult to top this offering. As Spinoza says: "all things excellent are as difficult as they are rare."

Glenn Statile, Ph.D.
St. John's University

TABLE OF CONTENTS

In the works that follow, George Stoukas attempts to present in a simple way, some of the biographical skeches and famous sages of the ancient Greek. His remarkable collection of these valuable adages, apothegms, along with meditations, wise sayings and proverbs are intended as an introduction to the wisdom of the Greeks.

His works about the ancient Greeks cover almost all aspects of their lives in several other publications.

His works were discovered by Dr. Sam Chekwas who has undertaking the difficult task of archiving them and translating them to other languages.

George Stoukas lives in the city of Ioannina, Greece from where he continues to write about the ancient Greek world.

Greece is not only the land of democracy, but also the caretaker of the mind and the soul of civilization.

— Sam Chekwas

PROLOGUE

Great men are creators of civilization, who through the charism with which they are endowed reveal the divine to many and embody divine truth and, as instruments of God, create History.

Humanity, from the foundations of the world until today, has many sages and great intellects to present, who literally correctly mapped out the life of the human race with their wise teachings, admonitions, discoveries, development of Fine Arts and of Science more generally.

Great men, then, are beacons of humanity, and for this reason their biographies comprise a field of study that inspires and ennobles.

Adages, says Aristotle, validate the acts of people, as well as whatever people are under obligation to do or avoid doing. In other words, they constitute a compass for a person's journey.

One can support one's thought on these adages and proceed to action in order to create, drawing powers from the powers contained in them.

All persons like these adages that are necessary for every human being. By means of these adages, one examines one's actions and moves on, having these as one's basis.

One is enlightened by them and with their light judges one's actions, as well as the thoughts of others, having the certitude that is supported on firm ground, since one knows that adages or proverbs, or things similar to these, are nothing but the highest human wisdom and refulgence of human experience.

The adages possess eternal validity and are given as if they were an order, a command, an inviolable law, like the ten commandments of the Old Testament, by someone who surpasses the limits of the natural.

One adage can contain the spirit of an entire book, of an entire theory.

The APOPTHEGMS we could say constitute the quick path leading to abundant knowledge, as well as the infallible mirror that shows a person exactly as he or she is.

HOMER
(9th Century B.C.)

Homer is the most renowned epic Greek poet known to all humanity.

According to one tradition he was born in Smyrna although many cities claim his birth. He live for somtime in Chios, and died in the Cyclades islands.

Regarding the epoch in which he reached his acme, there is no positive element to speak of. HERODOTUS (484-410 B.C.) places HOMER 400 years before his time, that is, in the ninth Century B.C.

Homer went about as a rhapsodist in Greek cities and sung epics. It is said that he was blind. This view is further supported also by THUCYDIDES (470-395 B.C.)

There are no specific sources in existence concerning his life, except for the known mythological traditions. Of his works there survive, primarly, two great epics, the first is THE ILIAD (he composed it in the prime of life), in which are described the different battles and images of the last year of the Trojan war (at the end of this brief biographical sketch, a few things about the city of Troy and the Trojan war will be mentioned), which has as protagonist the Thessalonian ACHILLES, and as co-protagonist the king of Mykenos, AGAMEMNON. And the second epic is THE ODYSSEY (he composed it at an advanced age) which contains the adventures of the shrewd and innovative king of Ithaca, ODYSSEUS, after the fall of Troy, during his return to his fatherland and his revenge against his wife's suitors.

These two poems, the *Illiad* and the *Odyssey,* are poetic masterpieces. They constituted prototypes for later Greeks and were used from the fifth Century B.C. as the primary pedagogical book.

The epics were written down and received their final form in the sixth Century B.C.

It is noteworthy to mention that these show differences between them, because there have been added quite a few myths from Asia Minor, many legends and mythical narratives, something which made researchers doubt the attribution of these two works of HOMER.

With the exception of the so-called "separatists" who regarded only the ILIAD to be a work of HOMER, and attributed the ODYSSEY to another poet, the entire ancient tradition accepted the two epics as genuine works of one and the same poet, that is, of HOMER, which, initially, were disseminated orally, from mouth to mouth, from one generation to another.

Thus was created, by German philologists, the so-called "Homeric Question," which occupied and continues to occupy the philologists of the entire world. This, however, in no way diminishes the value of the poems, nor the value of the poet.

The general perception that prevails today is that, on the one hand, the epics, as they are composed today, are the fruit of a long evolution, and, on the other hand, HOMER is considered to be the greatest poet of the ages and patriarch of the ancient Greek poem.

It is not possible for anyone who reads the above works not to experience shudders and to be shaken up from the depths of his or her soul, because in these epics, which constitute the most beautiful flowers of the civilization of the Greek world, there exists everything that warmly touches and shakes up the human heart – everything that is great, good and beautiful. The most sacred feelings: love of spouses and children, the family sentiment, love towards the fatherland and right ambition, constitute the basis of the works. We note, in particular, the beauty and modesty of the woman figures, as, for example, Andrmache, Nafseka and Penelope.

All these things give the epics a unique place on the altar of poetry, which I believe will be preserved as immortal, as long as human civilization will exist. And moreover, they have made Homer beloved by all the peoples of the earth, who justly consider him to be the most renowned epic poet of the world.

For the Greeks in particular, Homer was not only the father of poetry but also a teacher of ethos, a prophet of religion. The world of gods and men, heroes and women, rulers and peoples, animate and inanimate nature – all these are presented by him from the perspective of pure humanism. Only Shakespeare and Goethe, in a few happy instances of their lives, matched him.

A few of his meditations and views:

- Always excel to surpass others.
- Nothing is sweeter than fatherland.
- The volitions of men are one thing, but God orders other things.
- Of all virtues piety is pre-eminent.
- There is no living creature on this earth that is more miserable than man.
- Fools are destroyed by their own foolishness.
- All, sooner or later, will follow the same road.
- Noble spirits bend more easily.
- People who experience disasters grow old quickly.
- One evil always supports another evil.
- The prudent person always calculates before he or she suffers.
- It is honorable for the young to die on the field of battle. Such a death is preferable than for one to die old from cowardliness.
- Death is hated in all its forms, but it is more dreadful to die of starvation.
- The minds of the youth always fly in the sky.
- As much as you love your wife, don't tell her all your secrets.
- A ruler, to whom a state is entrusted, must never be careless or negligent.
- It is not right for you to refuse the present that they offer you.

LYCURGUS THE SPARTAN

(9th to 8th Century B.C.)

Lycurgus was a great legislator and social reformer of ancient Sparta. Concerning the legislature of Sparta, which regulated the manner of life and structure of the state, it is said that its inspirer was Lycurgus. Regarding him, however, modern research holds that it's about a mythical person. The legislation of Sparta was created in evolutionary stages and took on its particular form during the historic years.

At all events the contribution of Chilon the Lacedaemonian, who was one of the seven sages and lived during the 7th century, is considered a fact.

From ancient times, however, there were many contradictory views held in regard to Lycurgus' existence, life, and especially the time in which he lived.

We cite a few views:

- Today it appears probable that Lycurgus was a certain hero whom the Spartans set up as leader of the reforms.
- According to Spartan traditions, the state of Sparta was a work of the legislator Lycurgus.
- The historical myth places as founder of Sparta as a city, Lycurgus, who is as mythical as are all the founders of known cities of the classical world.
- Aristotle held that Lycurgus lived at the beginning of the eighth century B.C., perhaps even a bit before this, because he surely lived in 776 B.C. (when the first Olympiad was held) and indeed he must have had great fame since they placed his name, together with Iphitus, on the disc of Olympia, for which the Olympic Games were named. Iphitus the Eleion and Lycurgus the Spartan were designated as co-founders of the Pan-Hellenic Games.

However the issue might stand, the name of Lycurgus is connected with the reforms that occurred in Sparta and which created a new nation which enforced a more strict and frugal way of life upon the Spartans (the popular expression "he does it Spartan style" is not fortuitous), who were then organized into a permanent army. They reformed their city into a military camp. They changed their city into a camp without walls, in which all went through life with training and lived the same form of life, in what we now call a socialistic society that sacrificed the individual for the sake of the ideal interest of the state.

Structure of Spartan Society

– Political Life

In Sparta hereditary kingship was in force. There were, however, two kings, who descended from two different families. It was a characteristic mark for them to have many honors, but few rights.

Another political body of Sparta was the Senate, which consisted of 28 life-long members, the age of whose members was 60 years old and above, and whose origin was the most select families of Sparta. The Senate would prepare issues which would be discussed by the Apella, (a convention of the people in which only Spartans took part, who were above the age of 30 and convened at each full moon. The decisions were made by means of an outcry. This was something analogous to the Assembly of the Municipality at Athens), which tried cases related to murder and deliberated on issues of foreign affairs. Moreover, it had the right to judge Kings, when they were called in by the five (5) *Ephoroi* ("Overseers,") who, as it appears, were the real ones wielding authority in Sparta.

– Social Life

The primary characteristic of social life in Sparta was subjection of the individual to the collective whole. The overseers, moving on the basis of legislation, examined the new-born children, in order to gain certainty about the soundness of their members. The mothers kept them by their side until the seventh year, at which time they gave them up to the state. From then on began their training, so that they might become disciplined and very well-trained fighters. Intellectual cultivation was completely neglected. They would learn a few "laconic" sayings and battle songs. They showed a greater interest in developing certain virtues, as, for example, courage, respect for elders, and subjection to the laws of Sparta and to the commands of the rulers.

They would nurture the young girls too in an analogous way, and they took special care for them to become spirited, proud and brave, so that, when they would hand over their own shields, they could charge them with the known *'e tan e epi tas'* - "Come back with your enemy's head on the shield or your own". But the basic characteristic features of Spartan social life were:

- The Spartans didn't essentially own any land. It remained the property of the helots and the Spartans had enforced a usufruct.
- Each Spartan had a lot, which provided him with the necessary things for life and to be equal for all.
- Beyond land, every notion of wealth is prohibited, because thereby greediness is avoided.
- The law prohibits gold and every comfort in the home of the Spartan, resulting in Sparta being a real military camp.
- It is noteworthy that the law of Lycurgus does not prohibit the looting of invaded, occupied, or dominated cities, but rather the different kinds of booty are distributed canonically to soldiers. Thus the only source of wealth that remains is only war and invasions.
- Finally, all Spartan women had to eat from common kettles, in groups of about 15 individuals. This measure provoked many reactions and dynamic reactions.

– Military Life:

As we mentioned above, the children belonged to the city. It took them from the mothers to train them and to cultivate them in the spirit of the military camp and of the fighter. Constant, persistent training created a keen awareness of war, of the camp, of hard training, and of frugality in the conscience of the citizens. And in parallel course, it united its inhabitants to the common interest of Sparta.

The young men, at age twenty (20) were inducted into tents and from then on they now became soldiers. Spartan broth was their daily nourishment. At thirty (30) years of age they had the right to marry, but also the order to have many children, yet, very few remained in their home.

Generally, we can say that the aim of Sparta had been focused on the preparation of a single but well organized and battle-worthy army. The primary part of the Spartan army was the hoplite (heavily-armed soldier), each one of whom set up next to the other, constitutingd a solid body, the so-called Spartan phalanx.

The cowards they considered "dishonorable," shameful (the worst accusation during that time period). Everybody disdained them and they would lose their rights.

With these prerequisites Sparta succeeded in presenting a strong and disciplined army, which for many years only knew victory.

– Founding of Sparta

Judging from existing information, around 1000 B.C. in the valley of the Eurota river there was established the most dynamic division of Dorians, the Spartans, who, after defeating the inhabitants of the region of the Achaians, turned them into helots.

Spartan society was divided into three classes:

- THE HELOTS also had no political rights. They cultivated the lands of the Spartans and from their earnings they gave a portion to their lords (usufruct). When they drafted them into the army and they performed feats of valor in battle, they made them free citizens, "neodamodeis", as they called them.

- THE PERIOEKOI, who also had no political right. They would occupy themselves with Trade and Handicraft and were drafted into the army only as simple hoplites.

- THE SPARTANS were the elite of Spartan society. They possessed all the political rights and they took over all the offices, political and military. Naturally, their primary and practically only occupation was preparation for war. It was a harsh preparation that began from the age of seven years old and would continue throughout their life.

HESIOD
(750-700 B.C.)

Hesiod was born and died in Askra of Boetia. He was a Great Greek poet, father of the didactic epic, which is to say, he gave wise advice (he taught) about justice, work, agriculture, trading, navigation, marriage and the raising of children, with the purpose of ennobling the life of people or to relieve it of hardships. He was the first to occupy himself with the life of simple people.

So the poet was practical and versatile. We could present him marvelously as being like a collective instrument, which occupies itself with great success in all the spheres of organized society.

HESIOD is translated into all the languages of the world, and I think this says everything about his value.

His most significant poems are:

THEOGONY (1022 verses) in which the poet systematically records the history of the Greek gods and attempts to impart knowledge of moral and religious guidelines. Characteristic of his dialogue about VIRTUE: *"In front of virtue the gods placed sweat. An uphill road, long and difficult to tread, leads to virtue for the first time. Nevertheless, once you are made worthy and reach the edge of the road, from then on the journey is easy, even with all the difficulties that it will present."*

– Works And Days (828 verses) in which:
  - He directs himself to the judges reminding them of the evils that the trampling of Themis brings on.

  - He attempts to teach ways of dealing with life (agriculture, trade, navigation, marriage, etc.).

  - He advises on behalf of work, which he regards as the only path to human happiness, but simultaneously, as a profound exponent of life, he describes the human being as if he were the greatest psychologist of his time.

  - Work, he would say, is not shameful; laziness is shameful. The occasion for writing this poem was the brother of PERSES, who was sluggard and bad, who once having devoured the portion of his paternal goods, tried to grab his brother's portion by illegal means.

- From his work we cite a few verses that refer to man, and which, with the power of description, expresses harsh reality even today: *A day will come when children will be born with white hair and the father will not look like the child and the child like the father. And there will be no hospitality given for the foreigner, friend for friend, brother for brother. There will be no respect for the elder parent, nor a consoling word for him who has need, nor fear of God. Nor will children give nourishment from what they owe to their parents.*

In this time that will come, no one will keep his or her oath, no one will find kindness, neither the good, nor the just person. Only the vicious and unjust will be honored. And the coward will crush the manly by means of intrigue and will take oaths for falsehoods.

And then only jealousy, feeble, ill-graced, and with a dreadful countenance, will accompany the miserable people. Nemesis and Aidos will jolt earth from its place, hiding their beautiful face in veils.

And to people then, only dreadful pains will remain, because down here there will be no cure for the evil.

The above the prophetic capability of HESIOD is clear, who more than 2700 years ago, described people to us unfortunately as they are today. Thus, if someone isn't familiar with his work, they may claim that the description belongs to some great modern psychologist and philosopher.

Some of his thoughts and views:

- Don't put something off for tomorrow or the day after tomorrow, which you can do today.
- Just starting something constitutes half its completion.
- We owe most of our knowledge to our faults.
- Only the gods have no knowledge of the fear of old age.
- There will be no day on which the heavy toil and struggle for life will cease. And we won't stop melting from concerns even for a single night.
- Money is for us wretched mortals.
- It is a very bad thing for the son of a good father not to follow his example.
- Whoever loses a day without any benefit loses more than a day of life.

- When the laws are enforced justly for natives and foreigners, without any right being violated, then the nation prospers and its citizens are happier.
- Peace is the affectionate mother of Earth, and Zeus who foresees, doesn't send destructive wars to these lands.
- Both Gods and men are indignant towards the person who lives a life of laziness, like the lazy drones, who, without working devour the toil of the bees.
- Return love for love, and help him who helps you.

ARCHILOCHUS
(725-650 B.C.)

Archilochus is the most ancient poet of iambics, who descended from the most distinguished family of Paros Island.

His life was stormy and full of labors. While yet a young man he participated in a mission of colonization Thasos, which had his father, Telesiklis, as leader.

It appears, however, that in Thasos things didn't go well, because the colonists not only did not find the riches they had hoped for, but rather were suffering misfortune. For this reason, Archilochus was forced to return to the island of Paros. There he came to love Neovouli passionately, who was the youngest of the daughters of Lykamvis, with whom he also got engaged.

This occasioned the poetic vein of Archilochus to open in rich abundance. When Lykamvis denied giving him Neovoule as wife, the poet was pained and humbled. For this reason he began to insult and derides not only Lykamvis but also his presently betrothed, as well as her sisters.

The words of the poet were so poisonous, it is said, that, for Lykamvis to escape, even his daughters had to be hanged.

From then on, Archilochus because he was a restless spirit and not able to remain any longer without work in the fatherland, became a mercenary soldier and lived a dangerous life.

He took part in many battles and in one of them he threw his shield and ran to save himself. About this he says: "I'm sorry on the one hand that I became a *"ripsaspis"* ("shield thrower," a heavy and insulting characterization for that time, which signified the deserter and coward), but I'm glad I escaped death." For, later at a battle of Parians against the Naxions, he was killed by the hand of Calondas.

The Parians honored him, as God, and according to one tradition, the gods punished the hand that killed him.

Characteristic features of the poet:

He was a lewd, foul-mouthed, abrupt, mocking and offensive person, but no one was able to doubt his important poetic value.

Greek poetry, with its iambs (an innovation at that time, in which jabs and jokes were customary among celebrants during the course of a festival), went into a new phase. Thus, though prior to Archilochus, jesting, satire and bantering were self-styled and without artistic form, his genius formed them into artful discourse.

In all things, even in language, Archilochus innovated, for, instead of the existing till then epic style in use, he formed a language appropriate to the new form of poetry.

Archilochus was the forerunner of comedians and was praised by the Alexandrians as he was by Horatio (Roman poet 65-8 B.C.), who held him as model.

Justly, the ancients classified Archilochus after Homer, for, just as he perfected the epic, thus also Archilochus perfected the poetry of his individual feelings as well as insulting (scathing) and bantering.

Finally, judging from the different sources of information and opinions regarding the poet, but also from the fragments of his poetry, the emerging result is that Archilochus was in a class all his own who:

- Loved the truth a great deal.
- Didn't make an effort to be liked by others.
- Was somewhat harsh toward the "super-sweet ones" of his time.
- Had suffered a great deal in his life.
- Was endowed with much vitality and exceedingly restless.

All of the above is exemplary of a strong individual and great poet.

Some of his thoughts and views:

- For the incurable evils the gods gave patience to human beings.
- Disasters: at one time one has them; at another time another has them.
- My soul, you whom difficult concerns shake up, stand up, and turning your chest towards your enemies, support yourself, since you hold your ground firmly in the enemies' ambushes. And if perhaps you win, don't boast visibly, nor if you are defeated, cry at home, falling to the ground. Rather, rejoice a bit in joys and don't get too upset over evils. And, know what rhythm governs the people.

TYRTAEUS
(7th Century B. C.)

Tyrtaeus was a renowned Spartan, an elegiac poet of the 7th century. He was born in the Afnides (today's village of Kiourka) of Attica and was invited by the Spartans around 615 B.C. along with other noteworthy poet-musicians (Thaletas from Crete, Termandos from Lesbos, and Alkman from distant Lydia).

Tyrtaeus was not only a poet, but also a politician and military leader, who inspired and led Spartans, as Solon did a bit later at Athens.

With this general, the Spartans dominated Messenia and those of its inhabitants who did not leave became serfs (servant farmers of feudal lords).

Tyrtaeus was a contemporary of the Seven Sages, or might have even preceded them as he lived during the time of the 35th Olympiad, as well as the years of the Messenian war (645-628 B.C.).

The ancient sources are not clear in regard to Tyrtaeus' Spartan descent. The Spartans naturally were proud and considered him to be a born and bred Spartan. The Athenians however, as Plato informs us, as well as Lycurgus the orator, considered him their own.

On this subject, the Athenians told the following funny anecdote at the expense of the Spartans:

> That, when they were about to lose the second Messenian war, they were saved by a rogue teacher from Attica, whose songs woke up the lazy Spartans and nudged them on to victory. On the contrary, Strabon (a Greek geographer and historian 64 b. C. – 23 A. D.) writes that Tyrtaeus was a Laconian (i.e., a Spartan). Most probably it is the case that he was an Athenian. Thus such a view is accepted, at least by most modern Hellenists and historians.

Despite all these things, it is considered more probable that he was a Spartan in descent, since he was also a general. He gave orders to the Spartans, something that is difficult for the latter to accept from a foreigner. Let us not be forgetful of the fact that Tyrtaeus led the Spartans during the 2nd Messeniac War and helped with his passionate songs in the taking over of Messenia. The primary work of Tyrtaeus and the other poets who were invited was the composition of military and patriotic music (marches) and poetry, as well as the education of choruses that sung it. This would happen because Sparta was very often found in a state of war and had a disciplined military and politico-social structure and the leaders desired the population to be constantly in an enthusiastic, patriotic, and vigilant state.

Music and poetry were rarely taught individually to Spartans. Thus the choral songs (texts of poetry) that the whole body of Spartans of every age and gender would sing, gave the Spartans yet another opportunity for discipline and mass formation, because each voice obeyed the leader.

It appears that Tyrtaeus had a good, thunderous, and especially enthusiastic voice. That's why he sung his songs at public meetings and tried to transform the deaths that occurred in war into enviable glory.

The poetry of Tyrtaeus contains one and only petition: For one to risk his life for victory, going to the front line with the front liners (i.e., with those fighting on the front line). When he sings hymns he does it so to fulfill his petition in the present. With this spirit he also writes a hymn in his work "Eunomia," about the internal organization of Sparta as a constitution that is incorruptible and given by Apollo. In his poems again and again he makes the appeal to the soldiers to advance steadily, to fight boldly in battles, hand to hand, chest to chest combat, and to persist unto death, which is the highest honor for the fighter.

In order to form an adequate idea about the work of the poet, I think it is worthwhile to cite a characteristic extract from one of his poems:

> "It is brilliant, for a brave man, to die on the front line among those who fight for the fatherland.... Let each one stand on his feet, rooted on the ground and biting his lips. Let him hold firmly.... Foot with foot, shield with shield, let the wings blow in the air and the helmets mix, collide. Let the warriors fight breast to breast and each sword and spear mix in the clashing conflict of battle."

Leonidas, King of the Spartans, a renowned hero of the battle of Thermopylae (480 B. C.) would say about Tyrtaeus that he possessed the art of "tickling the soul of the youth".

A few of his thoughts and views:

- Sacrifice in behalf of the common issue can secure the reward of incorruptible fame.
- Virtue and real value in a man is secured only by the brave stance of the warrior before the enemy.
- In truth, it is a beautiful thing for a brave soldier to be among the first to fall while fighting for his fatherland.

ANACHARSIS THE SCYTHIAN

(7th Century B.C.)

Anacharsis was a renowned Scythian sage, who distinguished himself as an equal among the greatest Greek sages of his time.

He was born during the seventh century in Scythia (a little about the country will be mentioned at the end of this section) of Greek parents, but being nudged on by a burning thirst for knowledge, he traveled to various countries and finally ended up in Greece where he visited Athens (591-588 B. C.)

During his stay there he became close friend of Solon, who then was the legislator of the city.

Here we should mention that he ridiculed Solon, because he believed that it is impossible for written laws to stop unjust acts and greediness. The laws "the letters", as he calls them, don't differ from the spiders' webs: they catch only the weak insects, while the powerful ones break the webs and escape.

He traveled to many cities of Greece and Asia Minor. He became a friend of Periander (tyrant of Corinth) and his great fame reached up to the king of Lydias, Croesus, who invited him to Sardeis (capital of Lydia).

Anacharsis always spoke with courage and boldness, so that it became proverbial to say "speak like a Scythian."

Very few examples of his work which was mainly autobiographical have been saved. In the samples of his work that were preserved, his sharp wit and intellect is clearly evident in his answer to question posed to him.

Many Greeks (Diogenes Laertius, Lucian, and others) have studied his apopthegms and marveled at his sharp mind, the straightforwardness and balance of his thought, his sharp apprehension regarding human, and particularly Greek, things.

In one of his seven epistles, the fifth, filled with enthusiasm, he anticipated Cicero. (Cicero lived 600 years later)

Subsequent to the foregoing it isn't at all strange that in one of the lists that were circulating in Greece, he was counted among the Seven Sages of the ancient world.

Concerning his death, Herodotus informs us that: In sailing through Kyziko (an ancient city in Propontida) he saw a ceremonial rite being performed in honor of Demetra and he was so charmed by it, that he immediately swore to transfer the worship of the goddess to his fatherland. However, when in returning to Scythia he attempted to fulfill his oath, his brother Saulios killed him at some unknown time.

Some of his reflections and views:

- He was at a loss to understand how the Greeks punished those who hurled insults, but honored those athletes who struck one another.
- When asked – what is both good and bad, he answered: "the tongue."
- The best things, he would say, is to have one good friend rather than very many useless friends.
- The market is a place of mutual deception and greediness.
- When he once attended an assembly of the Deme (town meeting) and observed and followed the discussion, he said that among the Greeks the wise ones speak and the uneducated ones make the decisions.
- He was at a loss to understanding why lying is prohibited, since everyone lies publicly in the taverns.
- The people's enemy is their own self.
- Govern your tongue, your stomach and your senses.
- The prudent discuss, and fools decide.
- No one would get drunk if he saw all the shameful things that drunkards do.
- I am a Scythian in regard to origin, but not also in respect to my manners (or mode of living)

Scythia

Scythia is the land north of the Black Sea. The Scythians were hordes of fighters of Mongolian and European origin, who were nomads throughout the length of the Black Sea.

These bearded, stiff-necked savages, who were giants in stature, lived on their wagons, mounted their wild horses without a saddle, and their life was war. In other words, they were barbarians and lived to fight wars.

Every once in a while they organized invasions and caused great damages to Darius' nation (6th Century B. C.). For this reason the decision was made to organize a large army and fleet, for Scythia to be invaded and simultaneously Thrace too, where there was much gold.

Herodotus writes that this military campaign was done to punish the Scythians who would organize invasions into Persia with destructive consequences.

But the real reason was something else. Darius and those of his court wanted to increase the wealth of the Empire and simultaneously to secure the check-point of the Bosporus and the Hellespont, which would exclusively serve Persian trade and Persian interests more generally.

AESOP
(7th – 6th Century B. C.)

Was a renowned author of myths in antiquity. He descended, according to Herodotus, from Phyrgia (an ancient country of Asia Minor) and was a slave to the philosopher Iadmonos from Samos (he lived in the middle of the 6th century B.C.), who, when he perceived Aesop's talent, granted him his freedom. They say that they killed him at Delphi (the famous oracle of Apollo), or for his bad tongue that left no one unbothered (unbitten), or for being sacrilegious, because, according to Aristotle, he appropriated to himself valuable gifts of King Croesus (a very rich ancient king of Lydia, who lived in the 6th century B.C.), in whose court he remained (was offered hospitality) for a long time, after having been invited. As it is also proved by ancient busts which depict Aesop, he was ugly and misshapen. His primary characteristic was that he was distinguished for his wit, his bantering, and he worked as a comedian. He had a well-developed philosophical spirit and possessed a rare knowledge and keen perception of human beings and society.

These thoughts of his, which referred to the moral, social and political life of people, he channeled through myths in which animals were protagonists. And this he did so that his allegories would not be understandable to the many. Thus he augmented the myth-making genre that was known to Greeks before Aesop's time. However, he succeeded in making good use of it and in giving it a unique, unmatched form of perfection.

The myths of AESOP were happily transmitted from mouth to mouth and today are known to the whole world, where generations upon generations read and disseminate them with great interest.

A few of his reflections and thoughts:

- Fatigue is a treasure for human beings.
- Acquaintance softens prejudice.
- It is of no benefit to be alone when you can't protect your own self.
- Oftentimes music occasions salvation.
- Don't count your birds before they hatch.
- Necessity makes people innovative.
- Example instructs better than advice
- One should not adorn oneself with foreign feathers.
- One swallow doesn't create spring.
- Each person thinks in accordance with his or her interest.
- Riches always associate with the depraved.
- Concord is salvific for those who use it.
- If one would see things as they really are, one would not get lost easily.

PERIANDER
(668-584 B.C.)

Periander was a well-known tyrant of ancient Corinth. He was born in 668 B.C. in Corinth, at which he also died in 584. It is rumored that he was harsh to the point of cruelty and was famous for his capabilities and wisdom. It is said that he was called by the Athenians to be their arbitor in their differences with the Mytilenaens. Even though he dealt inhumanely with nobles, Periander was in all other respects a prudent and sober ruler. Thus, during his rule, Corinth reached the peak of its fame and power.

Periander zealously supported the works of peace, gave life to trade and navigation, and protected particularly the arts and letters.

He was a great reformer in all spheres: the social, economic, educational, administrative and political.

With his enactments:

- Farmers were obligated to live on their farms and to cultivate the earth. It was prohibited for them to go into the city without reason and thus much population remained outside in the villages and the farms, with the known beneficial results.
- He decreed various public holidays and began to give "allowances" to poor people.
- He prohibited Corinthians from acquiring slaves. Thus he secured a better social position to specialist workers than what this class of workers had elsewhere.
- Citizens were absolved from direct taxation because administrative costs would be covered by trade-law and custom taxes.
- He took special care for his citizens not to remain unemployed. That's why he created jobs. But primarily he began great technical works (markets, galleries, temples, harbor works, etc.) and he enacted a law, by which, whoever sat idly at the market had to provide a reason for it.
- He sent more of the population abroad, thus establishing colonies. The most significant of these was Potidaea in Chalkidiki, which his son, Evagoras, governed.

Periander was a ruler and politician who possessed strength, shrewdness, and great influence in Greece. This resulted in the development and cultivation of good relations with the Athenians and the tyrants Thrasyboulos of Miletus, Pittacus of Lesbos and Alyati of Lydia – with all the customary beneficial consequences that follow the peaceful and friendly relations of peoples.

He governed the Corinthian state for about half a century and justly became famous on account of the aforementioned, that is, his many and significant works in the trade, political and cultural spheres, which, together with the reforms that are associated with his name, served Corinthian trade, strengthened and empowered industry and shipping. He also helped the Fine Arts and Letters (in his court yard many poets, painters, sculptors and architects found special protection). It is characteristic that in his time Corinthian vases were in great demand and revealed wealth, power, and luxurious life, both the brilliance and civilization of Corinth.

Having said these things it isn't difficult to reach the conclusion that Pariander was a famous and enlightened governor who, with his varied contributions made Corinth one of the primary city-states nations of the Greek world.

In order to better appreciate the genius and wisdom of the tyrant, it's worth noting that he endeavored to open the Isthmus, but with the technical means of that time such a job was unable to be executed. At all events the fact that he contributed to the idea and purposefulness that this work would serve place him among the most noteworthy rulers, not only of the Corinthian people, but of the Greek realm more generally.

So it was only right for his time to praise him in song and to set him among the Seven Sages of Ancient Greece.

Some of his thoughts and views:

- It's a good thing for people to praise you while you're alive, and to wish you well when you're dead
- Become worthy of your parents.
- Pleasures are mortal, but virtues are immortal.
- Don't do anything for money.
- When you fare well you must be sober, yet when you suffer misfortune you must be prudent.
- Utilize (save, economize) your time wisely, because if it is spent where it should not be spent, little remains for where it should be spent.
- Be the same person with your friends, regardless of whether they are faring well or faring badly.
- Don't become prideful on account of your glory.
- Don't seek fame.
- Freedom is having a good conscience.
- It is better to die being frugal and economical, than to live in poverty.
- Not to offer assistance to your friend is like betraying him or her.
- All separations are painful, even those that we desired.
- Study everything.

PITTACUS
(650 - 570 B.C.)

One of the Seven Sages of ancient Greece. He was born in Mytileni of Lesbos in 648 B.C., at where he lived and died in deep old age, but it is unknown when.

With the help of the poet Alchaeus (A lyric poet from Lesbos, 7th century B.C.) he liberated his fatherland from the tyranny of Meleager and was appointed leader from approximately 585 to 575 B.C., in order to relieve the people from misfortune. Still however, slowly over time he too became a tyrant and governed almost dictatorially (a few things about tyranny and the tyrant will be mentioned at the end of this section). Despite these things he was distinguished for his sobriety and his prudence and his excellent administrative capability.

Pittacus was moreover distinguished for his clear and just legislation, and as legislator, together with his contemporary Solon are considered to be the first to enact written legislation for all socio-economical and socio-political relations.

He was a leader of the merchant and middle classes, but his program was conventional. Thus, though he favored merchants and merchant marines, he also adopted certain work-friendly measures. For this reason aristocrats became his adversaries and began to oppose him, organizing new conspiracies to end his tyranny. It is characteristic that the poet Alchaeus was now the most implacable enemy of Pittacus. His songs were libel, metered revolutionary declarations or slandred, insulted and derided Pittacus. He also organized a failed clandestine movement against Pittacus.

Pittacus, besides the gifts that we mentioned above, also had military capabilities. Thus, when the Athenians provoked the Mytileneans with war in the murderous battle that occurred near Sigeio, as a general he completely defeated and killed the Athenian general Phrynon.

Around 580 B.C. he willingly abandoned authority and passed the rest of the years of his life peacefully, having Letters (literature) as his primary occupation.

His favorite maxim was "know the time." From his writings, which were all destroyed, together with a treatise "On Laws," only a small poem of his was saved as well as a letter of his to the very wealthy King of Lydia, (an ancient land of Asia Minor) Croesus.

A few of his reflections and opinions:

- Know the time.
- Don't beautify your appearance, but be beautiful in your works.
- Don't get rich by means of injustice.
- It's a weighty thing to be uncultured.
- Utilize measure in all things.
- The true person is revealed when he or she is in a position of authority.
- Forgiveness is better than punishment.
- Glorify no man before his end (from his known epistle to Croesus).
- Necessity persuades even the gods.
- The prudent person knows how to successfully anticipate evil; and the brave person knows how to forebear without complaining.
- It's hard to be virtuous.
- Don't argue with your parents even if you're in the right.

THALES THE MILESIAN
(643-548 B.C.)

Tradition unanimously sees in the person of Thales the first philosopher or founder of Philosophy and considers him one of the Seven Sages of Ancient Greece.

He was born in Miletus (an ancient city of Ionia) in the 7th century B.C., with the more prevalent chronology giving 643. He died at an advanced age, around 548.

He was an unseasoned ("alatos") merchant, for which reason he made many trips, including one to Egypt, where he was taught Mathematics, which also constituted his great fame and glory.

THALES is the father of Theoretical Geometry, in which his proficiency and progress were such that very soon the student succeeded in teaching his Egyptian teachers themselves. Thus he measured the height of the Pyramids from the length of their shadow and determined the reason for the annual floods of the Nile were northern winds of the eastern Mediterranean during summer. He also developed many propositions (theorems) of which he proved a sufficient amount. For example:

- The diameter of a circle divides it into two equal halves.
- The inscription of a triangle in a circle.
- The equality of the two base angles of an icosceles triangle.
- The equality of the angles in an equilateral triangle "KORYFES trigonou" etc.

According to legend, the renowned Thales the Milesian brought to his fatherland the "seeds" of Astronomy, of Mathematics and of Geometry, after a long trip to Egypt and Mesopotamia (a land of Asia, between the Tigris and Euphrates rivers).

The astronomical items of knowledge that he acquired in Babylon (the land of the Babylonians, between the Tigris and Euphrates rivers in Asia) was later most useful in foreseeing a year in advance, the famous eclipse of the Sun on May 28, 585 B.C. (when the so-called epoch of the Seven Sages begins, who, on the basis of the most common lists, were: Thales, Solon, Pittacus, Bias, Cleobulos, Periander, Chilon). This prediction made him famous all over the ancient world and created an intense interest among philosophers for the Cosmos (Universe) and its extended aspects.

Thus begins the so-called epoch of presocratic philosophers, who seek the "formula" that will explain the Universe and to discover the origin of matter.

Some would say: The cosmos has been formed by four (4) elements: air, earth, water and fire.

FOR THALES, the primary substance out of which all the other ones came forth is water.

"The first principle of all things is water": he would say, according to a fragment of Theophrastus (philosopher of Lesbos 372-287) and which Cicero (Roman orator, author and politician 106-43 B.C.) reinforces: "Thales (said) that water is the first principle of things and also that God is the Intellect that creates everything from water." (See Aristotle's Metaphysics – Book I [983 b20])

- For ANAXIMENES (philosopher from Mili to 585-528 B.C.) the first principle is air.
- For HERACLITUS (philosopher from Ephesus 576-480), the first principle is fire.
- For PYTHAGORAS (philosopher and mathematician from Samos 572-500 B.C.) and his School, the Universe has been formed from numbers.

Finally THALES:

- Taught sailors to orient themselves by means of the Great Bear constellation.
- He calculated the distances of the visible objects from the steady surfaces of ships with the "simple method of the three."
- He was the "inventor" of the week (of the seven or eight days, we don't know for sure). He divided the year, determined its duration and spoke of the equinoxes. The result of these things was for him to produce a calendar.

Some of his thoughts and views:

- What has happened is certain, but what will happen is uncertain.
- Time is most wise, for it discovers all things. (With this maxim he presages Anaxagoras' theory 505-428 B.C.)
- SYLLOGISM: He would say that death doesn't differ in any way from life. Then someone said to him: *Why don't you die?*
  And he answered: *Because it makes no difference.*
- The most ancient of all beings is God. Without being born, He has neither a beginning nor an end.
- It is better for them to envy you than to feel sorry for you.
- Become a guarantor and disaster is near you.
- Love Paideia (education), sobriety, prudence, truth, diligence, frugality, art, and piety.
- Love your neighbor.

- I owe favor to chance on account of three things: first, that I became a human being and not a monster; then that I became a man and not a woman; and third that I became a Greek and not a barbarian.
- Love peace.
- Enviable is he who became happy on account of his children and didn't acquire official distinctions or honors.
- Associate with capable people.
- We must not do what we criticize others of doing.
- Necessity is all-powerful; it subjects all things.
- Don't ridicule the person who is suffering misfortune.
- The cosmos is most beautiful; for it is a creation of God.
- It is difficult to know yourself.
- Profit is insatiable.

SOLON THE ATHENIAN
(639-559 B.C.)

An important Athenian legislator, philosopher and poet. He was born at Athens in 639 B.C., wherein he also died in 559 B.C.

He belonged to a wealthy and aristocratic family and for this reason from his childhood days he was nurtured and given a well rounded education.

When he lost his property he turned to trade and on its account he made trips to Egypt and Asia Minor.

As a youth he was restless and a lover of learning, and for this reason he benefited from the many trips he made, in gaining knowledge and in studying the mores and customs, the civilizations, the laws and the politico-economical systems of other lands.

Having thus become intellectually equipped, when the right moment presented itself, he utilized it in the best and most effective way, for the economical and social restoration of his fatherland, and also in order for him to become distinguished as the most important Athenian man of his epoch.

The trust and admiration of his fellow citizens he won first as a poet, influencing with his flaming verses the Athenian public opinion, and expressing by them political opinion, advise, and encouragement, which enthused and touched the Athenians deeply.

He had diagnosed that the misfortune and quarrels of the Athenians were nothing but the struggle between the classes, that is of serfs (the poor and needy), of yeomen (farmers) and of knights (wealthy, aristocrats) and promised in his poems to cure the evil. He was chosen in 594 B.C. to be the ruler, and given unlimited authority to heal the societal wounds which then plagued the city.

With a series of more just legislative, and other, measures, he succeeded in practically equalizing the classes and in offering relief to the oppressed citizens.

These measures justly earned Solon another title, namely, that of reconciler.

Chief among these measures were:

- Disburdening debts that weighted down the Deme (cancellation of debts)
- The freeing of those who are slaves on account of their debts.
- The elevation of mortgages into properties.
- The prohibition of personal and family servitude (slavery) of the debtor and the improvement of loan terms etc.
- Change of the measure and coin system.

He also made significant procedural reforms like:

- The practical dividing up of legal issues of a political nature among rulers, whose decisions, however, were sent in disposition before the Eliaeas (the supreme popular court consisting of 6,000 citizens separated into divisions) which represented the Deme.
- Freedom to transfer property by means of the will.
- He gave the right to every citizen to denounce the ruler of the city for neglect of duty (prosecutor's office).

Despite these wise and saving measures which Solon instituted, yet still these accusations and complaints leveled against this savior and benefactor from each of the classes.

This state of affairs forced Solon to retire from public life and journey to foreign lands where he remained for ten years. During this time he visited Egypt, Phoenecia and Cyprus, in which he was offered hospitality by King Philocypros, whom, with his advice and seasoned experience, he helped to govern his land prudently.

When he returned, he passed the last years of his life in Athens, in which he defended and fought against the tyrannical dispositions of the ruler, Damasius, and died in deep old age in 559 B.C.

The huge administrative, economical, social and legislative work, which SOLON offered to the city of Athens, is great proof that he is justly classified among the Seven Sages of ancient Greece.

Some of his wise thoughts and views:

- As I grow old I learn many things.
- Praise no one before his or her end.
- Sarcasm sometimes signifies the lack of intellect.
- True happiness consists of the good life and blessed death.
- Happy are those cities in which the good are honored and the evil punished.
- Praise virtue.
- Avoid pleasure, which later births sorrow.
- When you don't see it, don't say it. And if you learn it, be silent.
- The person who can govern himself is capable of governing others.
- The honors that are obtained with labor are superior to those that are offered.
- If the accusing witnesses were not so angered at the unfortunate victims, fewer crimes would be noted.
- Even the most secret crime doesn't escape from the penetrating gaze of the King of the Universe. He knows how to uncover it in the depths of the heart. Sometimes he punishes it the same moment, other times he

puts off punishment. The punishment that the fathers deserve, at sometime redounds upon their children.

- When those who don't have injustice inflicted upon them are eagerly willing to hunt down and punish those who inflict injustice, and when this happens on a grand scale, then we already have the best system for a nation.
- Painting is silent Poetry and speaking Poetry is Painting.
- Don't become a judge of your friends.
- Many bad people become rich, and many good people are poor.
- None among mortals is happy.
- The excellent family is that in which its property was obtained without injustice, is guarded without lack of trust, and which spends without regret.
- Envy no one.

SAPPHO
(628-568 B.C.)

Sappho was a very great Greek poet, one of the first women in the world who wrote poems. She was born in Eresso, but according to others in Mitileni of Lesbos in 628 B.C., where she also died in 568.

It appears that, because of political differences, she was exiled by PITTACUS (one of the Seven Sages of Ancient Greece, ruler of Lesbos 648-? B.C.) to Syracuse in Sicily, where she lived from 604 to 591 B.C. and there they adorned her with many honors.

When she returned to the fatherland, she turned her house into a musical and poetic "Musopolon" school, in which she taught women, who, because of the societal and political systems of that time, were condemned to lacking an education. Thus she made her home a real school of education for young women, to whom she taught song, dance, poetry and manners, something that is missing from most, if not all, of our schools today.

As was natural, Sappho came to be loved with true devotion by her students, a fact that was misinterpreted by many men and especially misogynists and enemies of the spiritual and intellectual development of women. Thus, the poet was even accused of being immodest and provoked the bantering and sarcasms of the time and later of the lecherous Romans.

This opinion prevailed, without it being supported by any testimony, even until the Middle Ages. On the contrary, the ancients praised Sappho and regarded her primarily as a poet, as they considered Homer a poet.

Truly, what psychical power, what courage, what a moral figure and especially what a diamond-like faith she possessed, for a woman of that time! And what strength of character she must have had to change her house into a real intellectual center, providing entree into the male-dominated intellectual sphere!

As much as Sappho was accused, that much more was she admired and marveled at for her moral personality.

Plato called her the "Tenth Muse."
Julian called her the "female Homer."
Antipaters called her the "honor of women from Lesbos."
Strabo called her a "wondrous monster."

Later the Pythagoreans worshipped her; her fatherland carved her image on coins, and Pergamus and Syracuse raised the statue of the poet in their cities.

The works of Sappho, which were written in the Aeolian dialect, were divided by the Alexandrians into nine books, as many as the Muses, most of which unfortunately have been lost.

Today a few fragments are saved. But even these few relics sufficiently demonstrate the significant virtues of the great poet, whose poems were distinguished for their deep feeling, grace, guilessness, great emotion, simple language and especially for the perfection of their versification.

Sappho died in Lesbos in 568 B.C. and was honored particularly by the Greeks.

It is a characteristic fact that her statue, the work of the renowned bronze-fashioner Salanionos, was placed in the prytaneum of Athens.

Some of her thoughts and views:

- If a love endures, it's because something in us still remains unsatisfied.
- Friendship is the delicate pleasure of noble souls.
- The beautiful one is beautiful so long as he or she stands before you, but the good person is beautiful later too and always.
- An easy life offers delights and enjoyments. But I prefer honor to the brilliance of gold.
- Whatever is beautiful is also good, and whatever is good will quickly also become beautiful.
- We always love those who admire us; but we never love those whom we admire.
- The most admirable person is he or she who doesn't lose courage in times of misfortune.
- Sorrow and tears must in no way ever reign in the poet's home.
- Eros took over my spirit just as the wind surges upon the oak tree.
- That valiant one appears to me to be a true god, who, sitting opposite you speaks to you and hears you and smiles at you; for this reason my heart in terror leaps in my breasts; and immediately when I go to face you and for a little my voice departs and my tongue is tied and a smoothly breathing fire quickly runs through my whole body; my eyes blur, my ears ring, I break out in cold sweat, fear encompasses me, I become white as hay, I almost die. (to her beloved student Atthis).
- My children, you dishonor the good gifts of the Muses, when you say: we will turn you, beloved Sappho, into an excellent player of the pure, sweet lyra. Don't you know that my skin is full of wrinkles from age and my hair has become white? ...like the star-lit night, so also death pursues all living beings and in the end captures them. (to those who would not accept the fact that her passion had been extinguished).

BIAS
(625-540 B.C.)

One of the Seven Sages of ancient Greece. We know very few things concerning his life. Thus, from Diogenes Laertius (3rd century A.D.), we learn that Bias was born in Prieni (an Ionic city of Asia Minor in the Northern parts of Miletus).

The biographer Satyros (3rd century B.C.) considered him the chief of the Seven Sages. The Athenians had formed the same opinion about him.

Bias was famous for his sharp wit and his creative inventive capability. This is confirmed by the following incident:

When in 585 B.C., Alyates, king of Lydia (an ancient country of Asia Minor) and his father Croesus (a very wealthy ancient king of Lydia), were attacking the fatherland of Prieni and sent a herald to the city to negotiate, Bias, in order to create the impression that the ones being attacked could withstand a lengthy blockade and thus lead the king to despair, had corpses of sand made up on which he spread a light coat of wheat.

Here it is worth mentioning the following impressive fact: After the invasion of Priene by the Persians, many inhabitants left taking with them whatever valuables they had. Bias, though most wealthy and rich, departed from his birthplace city without taking anything. And when they asked him he said: "Whatever I have, I carry with me". This phrase remained proverbial in the Greek, as well as in the Latin, world.

Bias, however, became famous primarily because of his justice and his rhetorical capability. These virtues of his he used in order to defend in the courts gratis cases that were just. Demodocus informs us of this from the island of Leros, when he says:

> "If you chance to judge some suit, judge according to the manner that was in force at Prieni."

It is said that Bias also wrote 2000 lyric verses, in which the sage would show the way in which Ionia (a shore strip of Asia Minor between the rivers Ermou and Meandrou, where the ancient colonies of the Ionians were) would be able to reach a high level of prosperity.

The teaching of Bias consists in the form of maxims, primarily of a moral nature, as, for example:

Miserable is the person who is not capable of suffering a misfortune.

When his fellow citizens asked him, what is the sweetest thing to man, he said: "Hope".

"It is more pleasant," he would say, "to judge a case between two enemies, than between two friends. For, of the two friends the one will surely become your enemy, while of your enemies the one will become your friend."

Love as if you are about to hate, because most people are bad.

Often Bias presents himself as being disappointed and pessimistic with people. When, for example, they asked him what occupation gives the most pleasure to man, he answered, "Making profit" (gathering money).

Plutarch, Aristotle, Stobaeus and Diogenes Laertius, in referring to the wisdom of the man, observed that it was not so much theoretical as it was practical, and that it derived from the deep knowledge of the sage regarding human beings and their problems.

He was honored a great deal by his fellow citizens as long as he lived for the multitudinous and significant services that he offered his fatherland. But even when in deep old age he died (at court from a heart attack, as soon as he had finished his speech at some trial) the Prieniens buried him with grandeur and dedicated a temple (a sacred place) to him.

Some of his thoughts and views:

- I carry all my things with me.
- Obtain in your youth advancement and in your old age wisdom.
- Haughtiness is the obstacle to wisdom.
- Conscience is wiser than science.
- It is not indispensable for you to be wise in order to be just.
- Avoid getting rich unjustly.
- Hear many things; speak about serious things.
- The desire of the weak person, the lack of feeling toward the pain of others – here are two sicknesses of a person's soul.
- Don't praise the unworthy man on account of his riches.
- The honorable man should depart from authority, not wealthier, but more famous and more glorious.
- Equip yourself with wisdom from your youth up to your old age, because this is the most certain possession than all the other ones.
- The merchant lives in order to acquire gain; every other person acquires gain in order to live.
- The good conscience alone stands above fear.
- Make a critique of those persons who are present, but avoid rumors.
- Know what you are doing.
- Love just as you hate and hate just as you love.

ANAXIMANDER
(610-547 B.C.)

Anaximander was a famous sage of antiquity who was born in 610 B.C. at Miletus (an ancient city of Ionia) and who, probably, was a partner and student of his fellow citizen Thales (one of the Seven Sages of ancient Greece 642-548 B.C.).

He is considered to be one of the first great thinkers of Ionia (Thales, Anaximander, Anaximines, and Heraclitus) who set the foundations of Greek Philosophy, the first thinkers within Greek History to investigate natural phenomena and suggest materialistic answers to the question "What is the first principle of the objective world." For this reason too their philosophy took on the name: PHILOSOPHY OF NATURE.

It is very probable that Anaximander made many trips to the Aegean, to Greece, to Egypt and Babylonia. He studied Astronomy and Mathematics and certain authors mention that he produced:

- A solar clock, which, among other things, also marked the four corners of the horizon. Some doubt this invention of his because, according to Herodotus, this instrument came to Greece, from Babylonia. Perhaps it is most probably the case that Anaximander made it known and perfected it.
- A heavenly sphere and
- From information that he gathered from Ionian sailors he designed the first map of the earth; he could then be regarded as the first geographer. On this map he presented the earth in the form of a cylinder (an idea that constituted progress for his time which considered the world to be a round and flat disc), on which he imprinted marks where there were found Oceans, Elysia (an imaginary place like paradise where, according to the ancients, heroes dwelt after death – Elysian fields –) and regions in which various peoples lived. Moreover it printed the points of East and West and the path of the sun during the night.

Anaximander believed in an existing "undetermined" or "infinite" number of Worlds, that is, in the coexistence of innumerable "Worlds", analogous to our own. And in referring to the popular religious perception in regard to which the stars are gods, he attributes the Divine to the Infinite (and this is the Divine) which demonstrates that it doesn't constitute an "abstract principle", but an interpretation or a view of the reality of the cosmos in the dimension called time (according to the order of time).

He was the first to utilize the term PRINCIPLE, a term which from then on prevailed in philosophy. He had the opinion that the PRINCIPLE of beings is the INFINITE, which was immaterial and functioned by conflict between pairs of opposing two irreducible qualities, from which the worlds (the sum-total of heavenly bodies – the Universe) emanate and are formed.

From the ancient traditions we learn that he did not agree with the cosmological theories of Thales and, in order to confute his teachings he published a scientific treatise, which perhaps constituted the first prose work in the Greek language. *

Moreover, from other sources we learn that Anaximander called matter the Infinite, which he believed is something infinite and indeed in respect to space and time, and that it had neither a beginning nor an end (beginingless, immortal, undetermined, unaging, and incorruptible). And he added: "Surely there are changes and there will be changes, destructions, collisions of the elements in nature, yet, nothing is lost. Whatever is lost today will "become" again tomorrow. In the infinite there are contrary elements, as, for example, the thin and the thick, the cold and the hot, the wet and the dry." It is for this reason also that he accepted the notion that the material world was created from within the explosion ("big bang"), which is the principle of movement of various qualities of the infinite principle. Here we must mention that Anaximander did not clarify what this matter consisted of. This problem is among those of philosophy which the naturalists of his time did not possess the capabilities to solve, nor even to approach its solution.

For the creation of the cosmos (Cosmogony) Anaximander taught:

- How dry land and the sea were created. Regarding the earth which in the beginning was found to be in a wet state and later gradually dried and the mass was stabilized by the influence of fire that is contained in its dampness. Moreover, he also said that its highest surface is the level on which human beings dwell, and has a depth equal to it breadth.

- In what manner the Sun, Moon and the Stars were formed, he determined their size in comparison to the corresponding size of the Earth.

- That in the middle of the above heavenly bodies is found the cylindrical earth (that's how he conceived the earth) suspended, "held by nothing" which always maintains the same distance from all these.

---

* Anaximander was the first Greek who "printed" a book (a manuscript of which copies could be made) something which until then they considered to be a "barbaric" custom.

With this teaching of his Anaximander had a premonition for the law of gravity.

- How the beings (i.e., entities, realities) and human beings were created.
- How the principle of beings is the infinite which he considered to be like an inexhaustible reservior from which all things derive, and to which all things return because, according to law, all the beings must become corrupt and return to it.

According to tradition, Anaximander, when he remained for a short time in Sparta, forewarned the inhabitants about the imminent earthquake which subsequently took place.

Some of his thoughts and views:

- Whatever has a beginning and an end, is neither eternal nor without end.
- The stars are heavens of the same number, since each star is nothing but a brilliant opening, suited within a finger of air, sprinkled with fire.
- The principle and element of beings is the infinite...From it the beings are born and corrupted things end up in it in the proper manner; because they render justice and enforce punishment for injustice the one to the other,* according to the fulfillment of time.
- It is preferable that I sing so that the children will be happy.

---

* How they have been punished by mutual injustice, or how the same (the beings themselves) help to punish one another.

HIPPIAS

(6th Century B.C.)

One of the four great Sophists of Socrates' time, that is, during the first sophistical period (Hippias, Protagoras, Gorgias, Prodicus). He was born in Elis – a great city then near Olympia – and he was such a polymath that his knowledge surpassed the intellects of the people of his time, who for this reason called him "University."

He chiefly taught Astronomy and Mathematics, and his contribution to Geometry was pioneering.

His was a versatile talent: he was a poet, a musician, a rhetorician. Moreover he taught Philology, Ethics and Political Science. We can even say that he was also a historian because he set the foundations of Greek chronology with the compiling of the catalogue of victors in the Olympic Games.

So, Hippias possessed the broadest encyclopedic knowledge that assisted him effectively throughout his life.

It is worth noting that Hippias not only went about, as did all the Sophists, the Greek cities teaching for payment – the primary characteristic mark of all sophists – but he also became prideful that he obtained more money than all other Sophists.

Hippias became distinguished very early on for his great and excellent capabilities and for this reason he traveled to many cities of Greece and Sicily as an official person sent by his fatherland and as a professional teacher. Let us not forget that the sophists were roaming teachers and endeavored in this way not only to make their views known, but also to implement it in the best possible way.

It is said that Hippias knew so many arts, that he himself made his own clothes and adornments.

With Hippias the case is the same as that of the other Sophists. Because their works did not survive, we are obligated to draw information regarding them, almost exclusively, from the dialogues of Plato, who confessedly was an implacable enemy of Sophism (the art of the Sophists).

Thus we are informed that, in the assessment made of the sophists, Plato gives to Hippias the first place in the area of knowledge.

He particularly extols his knowledge:

- In Astronomy:
  "The Passions around the Stars and Heavenly Passions"
- In Geometry and Arithmetic.
- In Grammar, Rythmics, Harmony and Musical Art:
  "On the Powers of Letters and Syllables and Harmonies and Rhythms."

The philosophical work of Hippias was small but significant for his time.

It is worth mentioning how he protested against the perverted, as he would say, influence of the technical life of cities. He set in contrast – he compared – nature with law and called law the tyrant of humanity. In other words, he stressed, together with the other sophists, the distinction between nature, whose laws bind morally and are kept by all nations, and conventionality, that is, the customs and laws created by people for which he had no respect.

The result of this technique was to bring dissolution to tradition, as well as to religion and ancestral morals.

These thoughts, not only undermined the old props of Greek morality, but also encouraged many experiments in regard to lifestyle.

Thus is observed the phenomenon of "Chasm of generations" or "Generation gaps" in all its grandeur; elders, on the one side, lamented the loss of family simplicity and faith and the youth, on the other side, would seek enjoyments and wealth without the bridle of religious zealots.

Perhaps this reminds us of something today too?

Be that as it may, life continues...

Because, as we already mentioned, all the works that Hippias wrote were lost, for this reason only a few titles are mentioned by ancient authors, as, for example: "Discourse to the Young Men of Sparta," the "Trojan," "Synagogue," "Stromaties," and "The Naming of Nations."

Some of his thoughts and views:

- People by their nature are equal, but law, which often becomes "the tyrant of people," militates against nature in many respects and creates distinctions.
- Law can be "set down" for the benefit of people, "yet, if it is badly set, it harms."
- People often change the laws because the laws don't satisfy them.
- There are unwritten laws, the same in every country, which must have divine origin.
- Whatever "nature" allows is good regardless of custom or the law.

XENOPHANES
(6th century B.C.)

An ancient Greek philosopher, he was the founder of the Eleatic School. He was born in the third or fourth decade of the 6th century B.C. in Colophona (an ancient Greek city of Ionia in Asia Minor).

When in 546 the Persians took over Ionia he emigrated, and for many years he went about in the Greek cities as a poet and rhapsodist, in order to finally establish himself in Elea (an ancient Greek city in Italy) which the refugees of Ionia established in Great Greece, at which place he lived up until deep old age and died in 480.

The philosophical work of Xenophanes was destroyed. Thus we know what he believed only from certain fragments of his work such as "On Nature," a didactic epic, which would unfold his purely philosophical ideas, and from the testimonies

- Of Aristotle, who would say: "With eyes turned upon the whole heaven, Xenophanes declared that God is one."
- Of Simplicius, who attributes to him the famous saying "Everything is one."
- Of Theophrastus (a philosopher from Lesbos 372-287 B.C.) who informs us that Xenophanes believed and taught with consequence and passion that "One principle, that is, the One and Being and everything...for in this and everything is God. This whole being is neither limited nor infinite, nor does it move, nor does it remain still."

Xenophanes transferred Philosophy from the East to the West and gave it a purely religious character. Being a daring censurer of the polytheistic religion of the Greeks, he raised his voice against it and fiercely struck out against the cosmogonic superstitions and ethical principles of Greek Mythology. Thus he attacked with indignation the apprehensions of Homer and Hesiod who presented the gods in human form, lying, stealing and doing other similar sins which shamed the human race. Beings of such kind, Xenophanes would say, are creations of human phantasy. The real God is one and isn't like the human being, neither in form, nor in thought. He is eternal, indissoluble and immaterial. This seems to express a clear monotheism.

Truly, Xenophanes holds that no God can be governed by another God and that God is one and he is all eye, all ear, all mind, and he governs without labor by his own intellect. Since he is indissoluble, unmoved and present everywhere, he has no need to emigrate from place to place in order to execute His Council.

This one and only divinity of Xenophanes is harmonized with the Universe, so that his monotheism is also simultaneously pantheism.

From the above it also becomes clear that Xenophanes' interest is focused on the moral improvement of people. He said that gnostic people (that is, wise and knowledgable people), when they gather together, as, for example, at symposiums, have a duty to pray to God, in order to give them the power to be JUST. God, then, is a moral power; therefore Xenophanes was not only a philosopher, but also a theologian and a reformer of morals. Xenophanes loved life and joyful expressions. The most famous of these are his attacks against the Pythagorian myth of metempsychosis; he would say in this regard: "There where he was walking about one day, Pythagoras saw some people beating a dog, and he felt sorry for it and shouted: Stop! I hear the soul of a friend groaning from under the floggings."

His satiric vein would spare neither athletes nor victors of Olympic Games and he would say in this regard: "If this man wins in the chariot races it'll be the same thing; I don't care at all; our opinion is worth much more than the power of men and horses...it's not a just thing for physical strength to be preferred to spiritual, intellectual gifts."

Some of his thoughts and views:

- The Sun consists of fiery clouds.
- All things originate from the earth and find their end in the earth.

CLEOBOULOS

(6th century B.C.)

Cleoboulos was one of the seven sages of ancient Greece.

He was born in Lindos of Rhodes, of which he later became tyrant. He lived and reached his acme during the 6th century. B.C. and died at the age of 70.

Cleoboulos traveled a great deal. On one of these trips of his to Egypt, he came to know the Athenian philosopher Solon (639-559 B.C.), with whom he joined in friendship.

He wrote epics, enigmas (300 verses) and epigrams.

To Cleoboulos are attributed many of the famous maxims of antiquity, such as, for example, "The right measure is excellent," "Constrain Pleasure," "Don't do just anything" etc.

In Lindos, the tyrant produced many valuable works and gave assistance to letters and the Fine Arts. Among his works is included the renovation of Athena's altar, which, according to tradition had been built by Danaos himself (a mythical king of Argos).

Some of his thoughts and views:

- Like to hear many things but say few things.
- Don't condemn anyone.
- Be healthy in body and soul.
- When you prosper don't be prideful, and when you are in want don't humble yourself.
- Avoid injustice.
- The ungrateful person is a jar with holes; he or she accepts all the benefits, but pours them out into the void.

CLEISTHENES
(6th century B.C.)

He was an Athenian legislator, a reformer and politician, whom the Athenians in 508 B.C. chose to be their ruler with the command to complement Solon's legislation.

Cleisthenes, the great noble, was proved to be the most important political democrat. He strengthened the tendencies of the political policy that Solon had set down in the beginning of the century, and he is worthy to be called the founder of Athenian democracy, because with Cleisthenes the revolutionary change in the Athenian state became fully realized.

The social, administrative and state measures that Cleisthenes implemented constituted the basis of democracy and of social justice that prevailed in Athens. Some of the measures that were revolutionary for his time were:

- He made Athenian citizens out of the natives, of the resident aliens (the immigrants) and of the slaves, to whom in the meantime he granted freedom. In other words, just as Solon and Pisistratos granted political rights, he signed onto the registers of the demes many resident aliens (foreign members of demes, "heterodemotes," as we would say today in Modern Greek. This issue still causes us a great deal of trouble today, even if 2,500 years have passed since then) and slaves that had been granted freedom. According to his laws, citizens from then on were those who were born of a father who was an Athenian citizen, regardless of what was the descent or origin of the mother.
- He divided the inhabitants of Attica into ten tribes. Each tribe included citizens from all the classes, which were four, according to the census that was done then, not on the basis of property (Solon), but on the basis of money, capital.
- He ordained the Assembly of the Deme (the general popular assembly) as the primary governing civil instrument, of whose members were all citizens over 20 years of age. It congregated at Pnyka and voting took place by the raising of the hand.
- He restructured Parliament. Thus the Solonian parliament of the 400 was substituted with the parliament of the 500, in which each one of the ten tribes chose, by lot, 50 members each year, who were from each various demes. Among the duties of parliament, the most characteristic one was the preparation of law drafts which in continuation were submitted to the Assembly of the Deme.
- He conceived of the strange but effective institution known as "ostrakasmo" (voting was done with "ostraka," that is, with pieces of broken jugs). The process was as follows: Once a year the people

gathered at the Agora (a place of assembly), after the decision of the Deme's Congregation, which, as is known, made decisions regarding all the big problematical issues – internal and external – and voted against whichever individual it considered to be dangerous to the nation. Whoever received more than 6,000 votes was sent into exile for ten years, without, however, his honor and property being affected by this. For the sake of history we mention that the measure of ostracism* was put into effect for the first time in 487 B.C. and continued to be in force until 418.

- In 501 B.C. he reorganized the army on the basis of ten tribes and established the institution of ten (10) generals.
- He established two treasuries: one, that of the goddess Athena; and another, that of the Public treasury (State coffer).
- Finally, one part of his legislation was that which recognized religious tolerance and established democratic institutions in the matter of worship.

With these new measures and the reforms that Cleisthenes put into effect, the Athenian commonwealth was ultimately democratic, but not as democratic as it would become in the following century.

Citizens became equal and the state secured equality of civil rights and equality of laws. At the same time Cleisthenes succeeded in restoring order and tranquility in the city, which that time needed so much. Thus Athens was finally readily able to advance without distraction to the realization of her huge and amazing cultural work.

The reformative work of Cleisthenes remained the foundation of the Athenian commonwealth, until the city became developed. With these prerequisites Pericles in the 5th century B.C. succeeded in carrying into effect the most radical experiment of direct democracy that history recounts, because the office of the ruler, as well as the other offices, were "open" to all citizens, consequently also to the thetes (the poor class, the farmers). So Pericles was justified in confirming that:

> "If someone is poor, but can be shown to be useful to the state, he is not obstructed on account of his poverty."

Here, I think, we can say summarily that SOLON planted the sacred tree of democracy, it grew with PEISISTRATO and CLEISTHENES and spread its roots and branches with PERICLES they would thus created all the prerequisites for the coming of the illustrious Golden Age of Athens.

---

* Exile after the process of ostracism, of banishment.

CHILON

(6th century B.C.)

One of the Seven Sages of Antiquity. He was born at Sparta in the sixth century B.C. and died in 548 B.C. in Olympia from being emotional excess while kissing his son when he was declared Olympic champion in boxing.

They buried him with great honors in Olympia and on the statue that they had set up of him they engraved the following epigram:

> "Spear-crowned Sparta birthed this Chilon, who among the seven sages stands first in wisdom."

He was wise but at the same time he was a legislator who developed the system of the Ephors in Sparta, which played a significant role in the life of the city during the classical years. For the ephors had supervision over the youth's education and supervised the conduct of citizens. They presided in the senate and in the Apella (an assembly of the Deme in which only Spartans who were older than 30 years of age took part, and which would come together on each full moon and the decisions were made by shout. It was something analogous to the assembly of the Deme of Athens), judged practically all civil cases, and prosecuted crimes committed in the senate. Their authority had even been extended over kings.

In 566 B.C. he became ephor of Sparta and elevated the institution, making it a primary factor in Spartan life.

As was the case among many sages, Chilon was also a poet. He wrote elegies and about 200 epics, of which nothing has survived.

Chilon used words that were few, measured, and his phrase was always clear and without embellishment.

Aristagoras the Milesian called this brevity in speech and clarity the "Chilonian style."

Regarding the wise man we have the opinion of the historian Herodotus, who says:

Only one wise Spartan is mentioned from ancient sources – Chilon, who was the most intelligent and wise of all Spartans. He was the one who said the epigrammatic phrase:

"You guaranteed? You're lost!"

What wisdom, what prudence, but also what deep knowledge Chilon had in regard to human affairs is most clearly proved by the following answers that he gave to analogous questions, and also some of his thoughts and views which we cite here:

- When they asked him in what the educated person differs from the uneducated person, he said that the former "brings good hope."
- When he was asked, What is difficult? he answered:
  For one to keep a secret, to utilize one's spare time correctly, and for one not to become indignant when others inflict injustice upon one.

Some of his thoughts and views:

- Run to your friends more quickly when they are experiencing misfortunes than when they are prospering.
- Prefer harm to shameful profit, because the former will make you sorry once, while the latter will make you sorry continually.
- Don't ridicule someone whom misery strikes.
- Be meek when you have power so that your neighbor may respect you and not fear you.
- Don't speak before thinking well.
- Hold your anger: Constrain your anger.
- Obey the laws.
- Always be peaceful.
- Don't ask for things that are impossible to come about.
- Learn to set down order, or orderliness, in your home.
- When injustice is inflicted upon you, be conciliatory.
- Don't bad-mouth your neighbor.
- More haste, less speed.
- Don't let your tongue overtake your mind. (Think before you speak.)
- Pronounce happy the person who has died.
- Don't become prideful over your knowledge.
- Don't threaten anyone.
- Respect the aged person.
- Take your time when going to your friends' banquets, but rush to their misfortunes.
- Don't rush to speak.
- Don't love the person who is curious about foreign things.
- Virtue brings fame to the living, glory to the dead, and immortality in the heavens.
- Constrain your tongue. Particularly at banquets don't bad-mouth your neighbor, because or you too will hear things that will upset you.
- Zeus must humble the prideful and raise the humble.
- Don't bad-mouth the dead person.
- Guard yourself.
- Don't rush when you walk.
- Don't threaten anyone because it's an effeminate thing to do.

PHERECYDES
(600-? B.C.)

An ancient Greek philosopher, a writer of myths and author of one of the cosmogonic myths. He was born in Syro about 600 B.C. and died in Samos, in deep old age.

He established a philosophico-mathematical School and, according to tradition, had Pythagoras (572-500) as a student.

In his book "Eptamychos" (On the nature of the gods)), from which fragments have survived, he describes the origin of the world from the trinity of the eternal gods, consisting of Zeus, Kronos, and of Chthonos ("Ges"; Earth). He was acquainted with the seven sages of antiquity and especially Thales. He was the chief representative and introducer of the idea of metempsychosis, a view which holds that the human soul is immortal, passing after death into some other human or animal body. Aristotle characterized Pherecydes as a theologian who had mixed Philosophy with Myth, while many students distinguish in some areas of his work influences of Ionic realism.

Some of his thoughts and views:

- Time produced fire, air and water, and Zeus created the world from his cloak.

ANAXIMENES
(585-528 B.C.)

Third in chronological sequence among the wise Milesians (Thales, Anaximander, Anaximenes, Heraclitus) comes Anaximenes, who was one of the first great thinkers of Ionia who set the foundations of Greek philosophy, and began to investigate natural phenomena, while giving materialistic answers to the question, What is the first principle of the Cosmos (Universe).

He was born around 585 B.C. in Miletus and died in 528. It is said that he was the last Milesian student of Anixamander, who brought back into the forefront the philosophical question of Thales concerning the principle of the cosmos.

Unfortunately his written discourse has not been saved. It is, however, certain that in many things he followed Anaximander. He did not agree, however, with his teacher on the basic issue of the primary material-essence of the cosmos (Anaximander believed that the principle of beings is the infinite, without defining what that matter which constituted it consisted of.) He agreed more with Thales' theory of the cosmos, which defined a certain substance as the primary element of his cosmogony (Thales believed that the protarchic element of his cosmogony from which all other ones derived – is water.) For Anaximenes the primary element is determined, and this is air, which also has an undetermined (infinite) and perpetual motion. All of the cosmos (Universe), he would say, is air that alternately contracts and expands (condensing-thinning out). He understood air to be a kind of moving principle, which, as principle of the bodiless, is identified with the infinite.

According to Anaximenes, then, the whole cosmos is air that is found to be everywhere, doesn't ever stop its motion, but continually changes and is the cause of life and of movement in animate things. That is, he accepts that the movement of air pre-existed that of "eternity."

Just as Anixamander so also Anaximenes accepts that if the cosmos continually changes form, yet, nevertheless, nothing is lost.

In regard to these views of Anaximenes, St. Augustine would say:

> "He didn't deny the gods, but neither did he make mention of them: he didn't believe, though, that they created air; on the contrary he held the conviction that air brought life to the gods."

In respect to other considerations he first made the distinction between planets and stars and provided an "interpretation of eclipses".

He even sketched a theory about the rainbow which is due, as he would say, to the reflection that is produced by the striking of sun-rays on a cloud.

The views of Anaximenes became accepted for many centuries by astronomers.

Some of his thoughts and views:

- The principle and essence of beings is air: because all things come to be from it and return to it corrupted. Just as our soul holds us, which consists of air, thus the spirit and air contain the entire world.
- In the Universe was formed first Earth, which, however, has as its basis the depths of the infinite.
- The shrinking of air produces Earth, which is like a table that sails in space.
- The Sun is broad like the leaf of a tree and the stars have an earthy core and are supported on a crystalline cloud (a crystalline-like air).
- Air resistance determines the courses of all heavenly bodies.

ANAKREON
(580-495 B.C.)

An ancient Greek poet, who was born in about 580 B.C. in Teos (an ancient city of Ionia), in which he also died in deep old age (495 B.C.).

At that time in Eastern Greece life was full of extravagance, and poetry adorned and illuminated all the courts of the tyrants in Greece. Particularly the Ionians, during the time of Anacreon, lived life with rich banquets and erotic games, as well as with other pleasures.

The poet was young in age, when in 545, the fatherland of Teos was taken over by the Persians, and its inhabitants, and with them Anacreon, escaped to Abdera of Thrace, where they had settled in 654 with other Ionian refugees, the Clazomenians.

From his adolescence he was known as a poet and particularly he became renowned for his great intelligence, happy, reveling, and amorous nature, being weaned as he was in Ionia at a time of prosperity and full of extravagance.

The tyrant of Samos Polycrates, who was at his acme then, invited him together with other poets to his court, in which he quickly became the favored and confidant of the tyrant for whom he wrote odes.

The poet was honored a great deal in Samos and particularly by the tyrant. Indeed, legend has it that when Polycrates for the first time granted Anacreon five talents (a huge sum for that time), the poet, not knowing what to do, remained sleepless for two nights and at the same time was uneasy about losing the talents. On the third day, to escape the anxiety and worry, he returned them to the ruler. So money is nothing but trouble because....

Polycrates was killed by the Persians in 522. After the death of his strong protector, Anacreon was called to Athens by the tyrant Hipparchus, who was the son of Pisistratus (a tyrant of Athens, who died in 527 B.C.) and who had inherited from his father the love for poetry.

Anacreon brought to Athens the happy song and his well-written elegant art and charmed the Athenians.

He araced in song not only the court of Hipparchus, but other renowned homes too. Thus he became associated with Pericles' father Xanthippus (a general), Krita (an Athenian politician and philosopher, 5th cen. B.C.) and with Simonides the Kean (a famous Greek lyric poet, 556-468 B.C.).

The fame of the poet spread over the whole Greek region, resulting in his being invited by other rulers, among which was Ehecrates the Thessalian, in whose court he took refuge after the murder Hipparchus by Aristogeitona and Armodios (514).

The poet passed the last years of his life either in Teos or in Abdera, and he died, as Lucian (a sophist and author 200-120 B. C.) informs us during the year 495 B. C. at the age of 85.

The poems of Anacreona, according to the researchers and critics of his texts (grammarians) at Alexandria, were hymns, erotics, iambics, epigrams etc., but the core of his poetry consisted of erotics. Beyond these sweet, pleasant, and delightful works, the poet even knew how to create satirical works, like the one against the rival lover of Artemonos, which is characterized by its full sarcastic power and bitterness.

Finally, the poetry of Anacreon had a great influence and large circulation not only in the ancient Greek world, but also in the subsequent one.

His fatherland, Teos, honored him particularly and adorned its coinage with the poet's image. Moreover, the Athenians too erected a statue of him near the Acropolis near the statue of Xanthippus, which presented the poet getting drunk and singing.

Some of his thoughts and views:

- Drink and get entertainment; life is mortal and the time of our sojourn on earth is short; death is the only thing that is immortal.
- Eros is the ruler of the gods, and for this reason he tires people out too.
- Now my temples and my head are white, my happy days of youth have gone once and for all, my teeth are old. Not much time remains of sweet life. That is why I often lament, because I fear Tartarus; it is the depth of Hades, dreadful, and one's descent into it is a great labor. Yet, when one does descend, one can no longer rise back from it."
- I am inimical towards all those who are not openhearted and are sneaky.

PYTHAGORAS
(572-500 B.C.)

Pythagoras was a celebrated ancient Greek idealist philosopher and mathematician and founder of the so called Italian or Pythagorian School. He was born in Samos in 572 B.C. and died at Metapontio (a city of Italy) in 500.

Tradition has it that when the parents, on their honeymoon, asked the Pythia at Delphi about the children that they would obtain, she prophesied:

> *"There will be a child that will be shown to be useful to people and to all times."*

At a young age he heard the sages of his time. Ermadamanta (of Samos), Pherekydes (of Syros), Thales and Anaximander (of Miletus). These teachers of his opened new horizons for him, but none satisfied him.

At that time there ruled at Samos the tyrant Polycrates, who, after he withdrew its freedom gave it the brilliance of art and Asiatic extravagance and as patron admired philosophers and poets.

The tyrant foresaw in the person of young Pythagoras an emerging great philosopher, who was about to be a leading figure of his time, not only in the ancient but also in the more modern world.

Thus Pythagoras, on Polycrates' recommendation, went to Egypt near Amasan. There he remained a long time in the cities of Thebes and Memfida (celebrated cities of ancient Egypt), as well as in Babylonia.

Pythagoras, like all great men, believed his star. He feared nothing of all the things that led to knowledge and the fear of death didn't slow him down, because he saw life in the beyond.

When the Babylonians, and especially the Egyptian priests perceived the diamond-like strength of his soul and his passion for wisdom, they opened wide the treasures of their experiences. He was illuminated and cultivated by them. There he succeeded in studying sacred Mathematics and the Science of numbers or global axioms, which made up the core of his system.

Pythagoras was initiated into all forms of knowledge, gained entry into the Egyptian sanctuary, studied their books and reached the highest level of the Egyptian priesthood.

After a few years he returned to Samos, in which he wished to spread his knowledge, but he was neither understood nor believed. For this reason he went to Sicily, where the various Italian cities received him with favor. Especially in Crotona in 522 B.C. (the city was built at the far end of the bay of Taranta), where he developed, as a philosopher and mathematician, but also as a reformer of religious and moral life, a great active endeavor that very much facilitated the rulership of the aristocracy. And this was so because the teaching of his dogma that, in the state, the excellent person must govern, with the heir of sages as advisors, resonated.

In Crotona, therefore, he founded a School which was a mystical corporation in order to disseminate his ideas and to enforce the Egyptian system of monarchic priest-rule. In the corporation, which in all ways was the same form as the priestly organizations of the East, he would teach (his teaching consisted of various levels of initiation) among other things silence and absolute discipline of the initiated to the superior ruler. From his School came the saying "He said."

Pythagoras, with his excellent cultivation and the special aptitude that distinguished him in Mathematics, sought in numbers the primary causes of all things, either in musical harmonies, or in the movements of stars, in the nature of the gods or even in abstract ideas. The attention that was given to numbers provided a great impetus to Mathematical Studies. Progress was marked in Arithmetic, Geometry and in Astronomy. Here it is worth noting that his followers taught that the Earth, the Sun and the Moon are spheres. Nevertheless, these studies were compromised in that he attributed to numbers mystical and metaphysical powers that were foreign to true science.

In reality Pythagoras became very famous as a mystic and reformer of morality, despite his contribution to science.

Pythagoras believed in metempsychosis and taught that: "A basic prerequisite for souls to reach a higher position, in a future life, was their moral conduct in this life, in which contributing factors would be only Philosophy, Religion and Mystagogical Powers."

The School was of particular interest because it constituted the most noteworthy attempt of lay initiation and succeeded in transplanting the fruits of science to the tree of life.

Pythagoras was a mystic of the first rank, for whom we can say that:

- At the depth of his teaching shines the sun of UNIQUE TRUTH.
- He had direct vision of intellect, the key to apocryphal sciences and of the spiritual world.
- He drew from the true source of truth, the transcendent properties of the spiritual and dematerialized soul.
- He combined the observation of the psychical world with the superb classification of ideas with the help of his sublime logic and
- No one was more suited than him to found the edifice of the science of the cosmos.

Finally we should note that the aim of the Pythagorian Movement, among other things, was the creation of sages and virtuous men, who would be able to take on the rulership of cities. Thus, Pythagoras' opponents, with the noble and wealthy Cylona as head, succeeded in dissolving, by slander, the society (in 504 B.C.) and in killing or scattering its members. Pythagoras took refuge in Metapontio, where he also later died (500 B.C.).

Some of his thoughts and views:

- The square of the hypotenuse of a right triangle is equal to the sum of the square of its two sides. The proof of this theorem is given by Euclid (330-275 b.C.)
- All things are common use; let all of you have them.
- All things cannot be said to all.
- The totality of things, physical and spiritual – everything consists of numbers.
- As it appears, justice is square, equal and similar in all parts.
- Rejoice and appreciate those who criticize you and consider those who flatter you as being even worse than enemies.
- The lack of a good education is the mother of all passions.
- It is a worse thing to be a slave to passions than to tyrants.
- To silence the truth, when you know it, is like burying gold.
- Don't say a few things with many words, but say many things with a few words.
- It's good to remain silent or to say something better than silence.
- What did I do that I shouldn't have done? What did I do that I should have done? What should I have done that I didn't do?
- Whatever your fate might be, patiently endure it without indignation.
- All things are done by number.
- What is the governing principle of the entire state? Nourishment (that is, cultivation and education) of the youth.
- Those who are educated differ from the uneducated as much as rational animals differ from irrational animals, as much as one who has eyesight from one who is totally blind.
- Those who have learned letters see twice as much.
- Don't spend when you shouldn't, and don't be servile either; the best thing is to have measure in all things.
- No one is free when one doesn't govern oneself.
- Above all things reigns God, always unique and stable, of Whom it can be said that nothing is like unto Him.
- We must not derail a quarrel by means of nerves and anger, but avoid it by retreating.
- Be just.
- Choose the excellent life.
- The One is the governing principle of all things.

THEOGNIS OF MEGARA
(560-500 B.C.)

A gnomic elegy writer. He had a stormy life because as a noble he lived through the great conflicts and civil wars, not only of Megara, but also of many Greek cities. His struggles, especially in Megara, had taken brutish form. Everywhere the demagogues would stimulate the people and raise them up against the tyrants. Thus, in Megara, after the fall of Theagenis' Tyrany and the elevation to power of the aristocracy, the people revolted, and instead of them, established democracy in order to alienate the property of the rich, who were expelled from the city, and to distribute it to the poor. Also among those who were banished was the poet Theognis who, after roaming about in exile, wherein he found great hospitality, returned to his fatherland, where he recognized the regime and passionately occupied himself with poetry.

Theognis wrote many thousands of verses with moral admonitions and maxims, but few have been saved. They sung his elegies at symposiums, but later they would even introduce them in the schools, because the poet's maxims deal with circumstances that surround people in their everyday life.

Some of his thoughts and views:

- Hope is the only deity left possessing favor and good-will among human beings. All the other deities have abandoned us. But as long as human beings breathe, as long as they see the light of the sun, they rejoice in the good things of hope.

PISISTRATUS
(?-527 B.C.)

With Solon's reforms, Athens came to know Democracy for the first time, but neither the nobles nor the Deme remained satisfied with these reforms. The former wasn't satisfied, because they were limited in their rights, and the latter because the land wasn't redistributed. Thus, though SOLON gave life to the laws for 100 years, peace in the city lasted for only four years.

From 560 B.C., the Athenians were found divided in three classes:

- The *Pediacs*, who were people of the fields with aristocratic inclinations and were concentrated around Lycurgus, who was famous for his rhetorical power.
- The *Paralians*, who were people of the coast having Magacles, who was a moderate, as their head and
- The *Diakrious,* who were people of the mountain with democratic ideas and had Pesistratus as leader, who was a noble and cousin of Solon from his mother's side.

PISISTRATUS was a wise legislator, a reformer and tyrant of Athens. He was born at Athens, (unknown when,) where he died in 527 B.C.

It is said that he set up the assassination attempt against him with a dramatic entrance into the agora, since he took care to wound himself and the horses of his chariot. This, taken together with his successes in war, particularly against the Megara, made him beloved to the people and helped him achieve, with a *coup d'etat*, the power of tyranny, by means of the following very simple manner: the Deme allowed him to keep his own bodyguards consisting of "Korynephorous" (Club-bearers), for his personal security. After this Pisistratus obtained power and took over the Acropolis and became lord of Athens. Pisistratos achieved absolute sovereignty as representative of the people's claims and enemy of the aristocrats (nobles).

When he became tyrant he remained a democrat and had the favor and good will of the people. It is not clear how many years he remained in authority. Aristotle (384-322 B.C.) says that he governed nineteen (19) years. He didn't make substantial changes in administration. However, he completed the economic and social reforms of his cousin Solon by dividing lands that had been made public to small business people. So long as he remained in authority he truly conducted himself in a meek manner towards the poor and was a friend to farmers. However, he didn't keep his promise to the *Diakrious* (mountain folk) to create forests. It's a fact that he helped farmers with loans set aside for cultivation purposes, resulting in the increase of agricultural production.

He provided jobs to workers on great projects which he was doing and instituted certain good laws in the spirit of Solon, and in relation to these:

- He organized the institution of judges by demes (mobile agricultural courts) creating thus a new basis for the rendering of justice in suburban areas.
- (He taxed the production of farmers – the poor farmers remained untaxed).
- He removed from circulation the famous Attic Coins with the icon of the patron goddess Athena with her blue symbol, which helped a great deal in the blossoming of trade and handicraft.
- He gave impetus to pottery.
- Organized an army and fleet and surrounded the city with walls.

The foreign policy of Pisistratus was peace-loving, with all the known beneficial consequences that follow peaceful periods.

He built many works, temples, libraries, a new market and a sufficient number of aqueducts. Thus Athens was beautified by noteworthy works, among which also was the temple of Pallas Athena, which was built at the Acropolis, while at the same time work was given to many industrious hands.

He gave new life to the then annual Panathenias, which was the most imposing of the three great holidays of Athens (Panathenia. Dionysia, Eleusinia – at the end of this section, a little will be said about the festivals) by instituting the Great Panathenias (every fourth year) along with athletic competitions and awards for rhapsodists, who sung Homeric Epics. In other words, he wanted the city to shine with the radiance of arts and letters and generally he was concerned about the spiritual cultivation of the people of Attica. For this reason he called beside himself the famous spiritual people of his time.

Finally, we could say that Pisistratus, by thus strengthening the education of the people, was much more progressive and democratic than many others, who didn't know how to do anything else than flatter the multitudes.

Here is what he says on this subject:

> *"Beauty is created for the sake of people and the people are the ones who are benefited, not only by entertainment, which they enjoy for a few hours, but more so by the deep and delicate spiritual cultivation that they acquire."*

These beautiful thoughts, which differ in spirit from corresponding ones of other tyrants of the same epoch, is most evidently confirmed even by the words of Aristotle who would say:

> *"Pisistratus governed as a sensitive, civilized and intellectual democratic citizen rather than as a tyrant."*

For all these reasons, we must consider Pisistratus' governance as a transitional period which generally favored the progress of democracies that would later follow. With these thoughts we reach the conclusion that Pisistratus, though a tyrant was a creative and capable leader. In other words, he was a significant figure of Athens of the 6th century B.C. with a decisive contribution to its political, economic, religious, and cultural life.

Pisistratus died a natural death in 527 B.C. After his death his two sons, Hippias and Hipparchus, succeeded him.

SIMONIDES OF CEIOS
(556-468 B.C.)

A famous lyric poet of ancient Greece, who perfected the epigram (a small verse, particularly ingenious) and the elegy (an ancient lamentation form of poem). He was born in 556 B.C. in Ceos and died in 468 in Syracuse of Sicily.

Little is known about his life, yet from various traditions we learn that the poet distinguished himself in many parts of Greece, that is, in Athens near Hipparchus (a tyrant of Athens, 6th cen. B.C.) in the court of the Aleuades and Scopads, in Thessaly and later again at Athens, in the time of the Medes (the Persian wars, mainly during the time of 490-470), at which time he also wrote his two surviving famous epigrams below to those who had fallen at Marathon and Thermopylae:

"Athenians fighting at the Greek forefront at Marathon,
who layed low the power of the gold-bearing Medes."
(In honor of the Athenians who fell at Marathon in 490 B.C.)

"O foreigner, announce to the Lacedemonians, that here we lay,
having obeyed the common laws."
(In honor of the Athenians who fell at Thermopylae in 480 B.C.)

He passed the last years of his life, almost all of them, in the court of Ierona, the tyrant of Syracuse, where he also died in 468.

Simonides is the first who made the poetic art a profession. For this reason they criticized him, because he sold his poems to athletes and the powerful ones of the time, taking gold and honors for exchange. However, this fact in no way lessens his value and he is justly regarded an important lyric poet, rivaling Pindar (522 - 448 B.C.).

The poems of Simonides are characterized by diligence and pleasant expression, and they consist of elegies, victory hymns, dithyrambs, virginals, and especially epigrams and lamentations, for which he primarily became known and admired. Unfortunately, as occurrs with all ancient poets, the work of Simonides has been lost. Only a few fragments that the modern world came to know from German publications, which were done in Lepsia during the years 1863 and 1882, have survived.

HERACLITUS
(544-480 B.C.)

He was born in 544 B.C. at Ephesus of Asia Minor where he established a significant Philosophical School.

With Heraclitus of Ephesus, who reached his zenith at 500 B.C., Philosophy began to occupy itself with movement, change and the life of nature. Heraclitus held that not the "being," but "becoming" (evolution) is the basic essence of things.

Heraclitus is one of the first great thinkers of Ionia (others are Thales 643-548 B.C., Anaximander 610-574 B.C., and Anaximenes 585-528 B.C.) who set the foundations of Greek philosophy. They were the first from within Greek history who investigated natural phenomena and who first provided materialistic answers to the question what is the first principle of the objective Cosmos. It was also for this reason that their philosophy took the name Philosophy of Nature.

The denial of "beinghood" by Heraclitus and his persistence and study of "becoming," which he regarded as the only reality, led him to the theory, that an all-powerful cause, the "Logos," (Reason) continually reconfigures the changing phenomena of the Universe.

The personality of Heraclitus, full of self-confidence, combined with the evident depth of his spiritual perspicacity, has exercised great influence on global thought until today, though his difficult to comprehend words, the enigmatic and prophetic ones, together with his theory relating to the divine and human "logos" (reason) particularly emboldened mysticism.

Ancient tradition says that he wrote a treatise entitled "On Nature," of which only fragments have been saved. The ancients used to call him dark, because his writings were confusing and rough, but also because his style was very enigmatic and apocryphal.

Our time has shed a sufficient amount of light on the dark theories of the Philosopher from Ephesus.

According to Heraclitus' theoretical ideas of the cosmos, the cosmos is a single collection, which was neither created, nor shall be lost. The philosopher from Ephesus postulates as eternal and primacy element of the Cosmos (Universe): FIRE. In saying FIRE he did not mean only the flame, but also warmth (the quality of heat) generally.

From fire – according to his teaching – all beings are born and to it they return: "The essence and principle of all things is fire." Nothing, however, is fixed, permanent, unmoved: "All things flow, for nothing is solid."

The collective totality of the cosmos, according to Heraclitus, is like a river that runs eternally and which isn't found to be stationary for even an instant. An ever-flowing change is the primary manifestation of objective reality. Each thing changes; the initial essence isn't lost, but takes on such different forms and passes through different states; for this reason also he stressed that not only "everything flows," but also "war, on the one hand, is father of all, but, on the other hand, the king is the father of all things." Here he shows the war of the elements of nature from whose strong competition is born the life and harmony of the Universe (Cosmos).

This unceasing change occurs everywhere in nature and in society. Tranquility and motionlessness cannot exist in nature because these conditions are seen only among dead organisms.

Heraclitus, in contradistinction to the Eleatic philosophers, who had held the view that the complete immobility of "beinghood," declared with passion and self-confidence that, without movement life and evolution cannot exist. And since all things are in flux, and since nothing remains perfectly stable and unchanging, all things move; there is eternal change: "All things are ever becoming and changing, and nothing remains the same."

Finally, Heraclitus was a dialectician and a materialist. He didn't believe in extraterrestrial and supernatural powers. He recommended self-governance and obedience to the laws, and considered keeping the right measure in all things to be the greatest virtue.

After the above considerations we may say that Heraclitus possessed a universal intellect and his philosophy constitutes a unique view of the world.

The modern world considers him, together with Democritus, the forerunner of the Natural Sciences and of our Atomic Age.

Some of his thoughts and views:

- War is the father of all and strife the mother of all (he means the continual friction and colliding of the natural elements).
- Everything is in flux, for nothing is stable.
- All things are advancing and nothing remains stationary.
- This world, being the same always, is neither made by a god nor human being. But, it always existed and exists and shall exist, an immortal fire, which lights up and extinguishes periodically.
- You can't take two gulps of water from the same river and have both gulps be the same.
- You won't find the ends (the boundaries) of the soul.
- For me one true human being is equivalent to many thousands of human beings, while among the multitudes there is not one.
- Neither can that great Sun come out of its preordained orbit.
- People must fight on behalf of law, as it fights for the support of its walls.

ARISTIDES THE JUST

(540-468 B.C.)

Aristides the Athenian general and politician. He was born in 540 B.C. at Athens, where he also died, very poor, in 468.

He participated in the reformation of the Solonian Commonwealth that Cleisthenes put into effect (an Athenian politician) in 509 B.C.

At the battle of Marathon (490 B.C.) he was one of the generals who directed the victorious battle of the Greeks against the Persians.

The following year he (489) he was declared ruler of the Athenians.

As a politician he possessed a political philosophy that was contrary to that of Themistocles, who, as it is known, had worked out a naval program for the production of a great fleet (he thought that thus Athens would be saved); and this, because he feared that this would contribute to the neglect of agriculture (he represented the agricultural population).

The result of his this resistance was for him to be banished in 483 B.C. However, with the impending naval battle of Salamina he returned, took part and distinguished himself in the taking over of the small island of Psyttalea, where many Persians were killed in that mortal battle.

In 479 he was general of the Athenians at the victorious battle of Plateon.

After the end of the (Persian) wars he becomes a helper and supporter of Themistocles in the work of fortifying the city by means of the raising of walls, and he proposed the elevation of citizens of all social classes to official state positions.

In addition to his great love of country, ARISTIDES was most distinguished for his prudence and especially his strict justice, virtues that he demonstrated particularly as leader of the Athenian fleet that sailed in Asia Minor.

For the virtues mentioned above he was surnamed "the righteous."

After his death the state honored him specially and because he died very poor it provided dowry for his daughters and strengthened his son economically.

Some of his thoughts and views:

- Virtue is not lost when one dies.
- The most beloved thing to a person is his or her paternal land.
- If possible, seek peace, but spare no effort in enforcing justice.
- No one is as good as one ought to be.
- For those who do the good, life is short, but for those who do evil, even a single night is an infinite period of time.

- In a time of anarchy might is the measure of what is right.
- The family is the basis and principle (starting point) of every civilization.
- It is better for many, and not just for one, to see.
- When one distributes his property to his enemies and slanderers, this makes life unlivable.
- It is difficult to execute an action, but it's easy to give an order.
- Laws want and seek what is just, what is good, and what is to our interest.

EPIMARCHUS
(540-450 B.C.)

Epimarchus was a philosopher and poet comedian. He was born in Cos. As a youth he moved to Megara in Sicily and then to Syracuse, where the tyrants Gelon and Ieron, who were cultivated and lovers of the muses, encouraged dramatical and musical contests at the great theatre that they had built. This contributed to the development of the great poetic genius of Epimarmos, whom the Syracusians loved particularly and honored with a statue.

He simply satirized human faults and especially foolishness and the absurd things that occur in all social classes. Epimarchus was the first to satirize the drunk. Aside from his significant theatrical abilities the poet also displayed philosophical inclinations, was highly educated and was influenced by Pythagorian philosophy. For this reason also his comedies are full of philosophical ideas and maxims, that were directed not only to issues of morality, but also to metaphysical problems, as, for example, theogony, the creation of the world, and the soul, etc. To Epimarchus are attributed 36 to 52 comedies, whose content can only be compared to the tragedies of Euripides. Plato considers Epimarchus a leading figure among comedians, as well as among philosophers, on account of the philosophical views with which he sprinkled all his works, from which unfortunately, as occurs with practically all ancient philosophers, only fragments have been saved.

Some of his thoughts and views:

- The wise person is in duty bound not to repent, but to foresee.
- It is the mind that sees and hears; the other faculties, or powers, are deaf and dumb.

PHOCYLIDES
(537 B.C.)

Phocyclides was a gnomic poet from Miletus who reached his zenith during 537 B.C. He sparred in verses back and forth with his contemporary, Demodocos, from Leros, who was also a poet. He wrote moral canons in hexameters and couplets which he began firmly with: "And this is to Phocylides." One great poem of Admonition consisting of 200 hexameters, which has survived complete and which is called "Phocylidea," doesn't belong to him, but to Jewish Alexandrian poet with the same name, who lived between the 2nd century B.C. and the imperial rule of Nero.

A few of his thoughts and views:

- Work and live by means of your labor. It is a natural consequence for every idle person to either steal in order to be nourished, or to gather the crumbs from a foreign table. If you haven't learned an art, dig with a two-pointed mattock. All jobs are part of the lot of life. Become a sailor, the sea is broad.
- And this is to Phocylides: reason is a weapon that is more penetrating than iron.
- Gold, ruler of evil people, corrupter of all, it would have been better for mortals not to have invented you; for on account of you battles are fought, plunderings and murders are done; on account of you parents and children become enemies and those with the same blood hate one another.
- Don't inflict injustice on others if you don't want injustice to be inflicted on you.
- Don't feel sorry for your riches; remember that you are mortal.

THEMISTOCLES
(525-460 B.C.)

Themistocles was a very great politician, general, and admiral of the ancient Athenians. To him was due the freedom of the Greeks, and the acme and glory of Athens at the beginning of the 5th century B.C. He prepared the road for PERICLES and sowed the seed so that the fragrant flower of the "Golden Age" might blossom.

He was born at about 525 B.C. at Athens and died at Magnesia (a city on the Meandric river of Asia Minor) in 460, at the age of 65 years old, according to some by natural death, and according to others he committed suicide.

His descent was not aristocratic. He was active, was able to see far, had excellent organizational capabilities that helped him distinguish himself as an ingenious politician. Here it is worth citing the action of his father, who, when he realized that his son was passionately going in the direction of politics, took him to the beach and would show him the triremes that were thrown onto the sand, saying "thus do the people conduct themselves also towards their political leaders, when they don't need them anymore" (prophetic were the words of his father. Themistocles would die banished in foreign lands). Themestocles, however, had set down his path. With his intelligence, his devotion to democracy, with his many spiritual and natural gifts and his eloquence he rose up high and became a politician whom his friends admired. Thus he distinguished himself early in life and at the age of 33 he was chosen General (490).

THUCYDIDES (470-395 B.C.) described him as a great politician. "Themistocles – he writes – was a man who presented most brilliantly the signs of a great genius, and for this reason he is worthy of great admiration, more than any other...

He possessed the ability to judge, perfectly foreseeing what was to one's interest from what was harmful, even though this yet remained in the darkness of the future. Generally he was very capable of conceiving the appropriate strategies by means only of his great genius, without much study."

From the moment he took on the office of Ruler he had already set down the initial foundations of his ingenious work. He understood well the value of the port of Peraia, along with two natural ports of Zeas and Mounichia and began to fortify them. From then Peraias became a large port, which in the years of its prosperity served the Athenian Democracry from the economical, military, and political perspective. Following this he turned the Athenians' attention toward the sea and thus prepared for the naval glory of Athens.

On this issue, PLUTARCH (127-46 B.C.) writes: "Themistocles began slowly to inspire in the Athenians a love for creating a naval fleet because, according to his opinion, they couldn't even adequately deal with their neighbors with only the infantry, while with their naval fleet they would be enabled both to fight the barbarians and to govern Greece." Concerning the same subject Thucydides, who was closer to the events, stresses that Themistocles was telling the Athenians: "Do you want to become strong and have others take you into account seriously? The best thing you can do is to create a naval fleet."

In continuation Themistocles worked out a significant naval program for the production of a great fleet, to which Aristides (540-468 B.C.) reacted negatively, because he feared that this would contribute to the neglect of agriculture Aristides was a representative of the agricultural population, but in the end, not only did Themistocles enforce his will, but he succeeded in sending Aristedes (483) into exile.

After this he ingeniously interpreted the oracle that the Delphic oracle of Apollo had given and which said that the Athenians had to entrust their fate to the "wooden walls" that girded the Acropolis. So, according to that interpretation of the oracle the Athenians found refuge in this. Nevertheless, Themistocles declared that the oracle referred to the fleet and persuaded most of the Athenians to abandon their homes and to take refuge in Salamina, Aegina, and Troezene.

After the battle of Marathon (490) in which he took part, and because he knew that the war with the Persians not only was not over but had just begun, he proposed – and it was accepted – a vote in 487, by which the profits of the mines of Lavrio, which then were being distributed to the people, would be used for creating battle ships.

200 new ships were built, of a new type, which were called triremes and had three rows of oars.

The building of such a strong fleet (200 new and 100 old ships) had multiple consequences, which were:

- It made Athens into a great naval power, which could compete even with the Phoenecians, who were the rulers of the Mediterranean.
- Athenian Democracy from here on in entrusts it future to the sea.
- It transposed the Athenian Economy towards navigation and Trade at the expense of the Agricultural Economy (so Aristides was right in feeling uneasy about this).

The events that followed vindicated Themistocles.

History made its judgment, that Themistocles's plan carries the seal of his great genius.

The naval battle of Salamina and the glorious victory of the Greek fleet is attributed to him (September 480 B.C.), so much so because he had the inspiration and keen insight to create a powerful fleet, and because he drew away the Persians into the straits of Salamina and with artistry and shrewdness (he set up all the Ionians as suspects for the Persians and followed them in the campaign against the Greeks. In parallel course, he sent his slave Sikinno to Xerxes to inform him that the Greeks were retreating) he forced them to engage in naval battle and to be destroyed.

These historical events had, among other things, as a result, full recognition by all that Themistocles was the savior of their fatherland and for this reason it is said that, in the Olympic games, the eyes of all those present were turned towards him, rather than towards the competing athletes.

Finally in 479, after his proposal, he began to build around the city of Athens a wall that even took his name.

However, as it usually occurs with great men, so also Themistocles was envied by the Spartans, but even in Athena itself he was considered dangerous, since he had become all-powerful. Indeed the Spartans, in order to completely take him out, didn't hesitate to criticize him as a co-worker of the betrayer Pausanias.

This slanderous campaign concluded in Themistocles being condemned around 471 it exile, something that was due to the great power of Kimon (an Athenian politician and military officer 510-449 B.C.).

Thus he passed into Asia Minor and reached Sousa (capital of ancient Persia) up to Artaxerxes, the King of the Persians and from there reached Magnesia of Maiandros, where he also died in 460, according to some by natural death, and according to others by suicide, because he didn't want to lead the Persians against Greece, like a new Demaratos.

Some of his thoughts and views:

- Miltiades' glory doesn't let me sleep.
- You might strike first but you will hear it later.
- Only the wooden walls will save the Athenians.
- It's impossible for the innate character of the black-yellow fox or the roaring lion to change.
- The wildest colts become excellent horses when they are educated properly.

AESCHYLUS
(525-456 B.C.)

The father of Greek tragedy and the greatest of tragedians. He was of aristocratic descent.

He was born and nurtured in Eleusina, where he was influenced much by the religion of the mysteries performed there. Thus, his descent, the religion and the free political spirit that he possessed, contributed so that the ethos of the poet may be formed sublime, brave and pious. This is also why he participated in all the contests of the State in behalf of freedom, at Marathon, where, fighting heroically he was wounded, at Artemesio, Salamina and Plataies. His poetry images the brave and proud mind-set of the Marathon fighter and sings of the liberators of Greece.

He is par excellence the representative of the pure, pious and courageous generation of Marathon-fighters, in whose name, says Demosthenes, he would swear "by the warriors of Marathon."

He is the man of thought and of action and a lauder of great ancient virtues: of prudence, of conscience, of honor and of measure.

He wrote 70-90 tragedies and dramas and he exercised his dramatic art as a profession.

His first work saw the stage in 500 B.C., that is, when he was 25 years old, but his first victorious play was staged in 484. From then on until 468 he was the only hero of theatre. That year he was defeated by Sophocles who at that time whose work was making his its appearance in the theatre. From then on one would win at one time, and at another time the other.

Aeschylus' greatest advantage is his poetic genius. The works that he wrote are more in the nature of divine gifts than creations of art. From his tragedies that have survived and which are known to the whole world, Aeschyslus truly convinces us that he is the greatest tragic poet of the ancient world, who is irrepeatable in greatness, power and prophetic vision.

From the dramas of Aeschylus there were saved only seven (7) tragedies and many fragments of other ones. All the tragedies predate the naval battle of Salamina and are the following:

1. THE PERSIANS (472), a tragedy that was written in order to sing the praises of victory of the Greeks against the Persians at Salamina.
   Let us keep in mind, however, the victory songs that the Greeks warriors sung during the naval battle:

> *"Children of the Greeks, go forward, free the fatherland, free the children, the women and the altars of the gods of our fathers and the tombs of our forefathers."*

2. THE SEVEN AGAINST THEBES (467), where the hero of the tragedy,
   ETEOCLES, inspires the army of the city for the decisive defense against the coming enemies, of which seven (7) generals were found before the walls of the city.
3. THE SUPPLIANT WOMEN, who are, perhaps, the oldest of all tragedies that have been saved and in which are imaged the civilization of the Greeks, in contradistinction with the violence and bad behavior of the barbarous peoples of Asia and of Africa, whose bad deportment is analogously condemned.
4. PROMETHEUS BOUND was the middle tragedy of the trilogy, of which the first was PROMETHEUS THE FIRE-BEARER, and third PROMETHEUS UNBOUND.
5. **6. and** 7. THE THREE tragedies AGAMEMNON, THE LIBATION BEARERS, and the EUMENIDES constitute the trilogy which is called ORESTEIA which is most grandiose, after the ILIAD and the ODYSSEY, a monument of Greek letters (458).

Some of his thoughts and views:

- Right thinking constitutes a gift of God.
- Riches in no way benefit the dead.
- Time, which ages us, teaches us all things.
- Who else, other than the gods, passes his eternity without tortures?
- The gods take care to provide for whatever is necessary.
- Time annihilates everything, since it grows old with them.
- Respect neither anarchy nor despotism.
- Wise is the person who knows but does not consider the many things useful.
- Few are those people who have the innate disposition to honor their happy friend, without envy.
- People are formed to trample on the one who has fallen.
- Justice isn't suited to family relations.
- Great trust and confidence can harm us.
- What we desire in our youth reaches us abundantly in our old age.
- The prudent, just, good man must be silent and only say the necessary things.
- Pain is relieved with tears.

- Justice shines even in poor homes and honors the pious; it disdains the shining brilliance of gold that has been obtained with dirty hands, because it has become accustomed to going near holiness and not to bow to riches. Justice judges each action proportionately.
- Disaster similarly often visits the one at one time, and the other at another time.
- It is the sweetest thing to journey on the path of long life with bold hope.
- Happiness is for human beings something more than a divine gift.
- There is no power in thought when it takes the wrong path.
- Good actions are born from discipline.

PINDAR
(522-448 B.C.)

Pindar was born in 522 B.C. at Kynos Kephales of Thebes and died in deep old age, probably in 448, at Argos.

He was the greatest lyric poet of ancient Greece. At the age of 20 years old he made his appearance as a poet to the common populace.

The great achievements of Greeks against the Persians strangely didn't move or touch him spiritually as they did Aeschylus and Simonides. And this is due to the political orientation of his fatherland in general. Later, however, he sanf of the brilliant accomplishments of the Athenians throughout Greece, and the Athenians honored him and granted him thousands of drachmas.

Very quickly the fame of the poet was disseminated so that he might receive the characterization of National poet, like Simonides (556-468). In this regard what contributed a great deal were the Panhellenic contests (they were held with special brilliance at that time), which he connected with the noble homes of all the cities. Many times indeed he accompanied the victorious athletes to their particular fatherland in order for he himself to direct there the victorious procession of their reception.

He always had close relations with the Priesthood and particularly with the priests of Delphi, whose wisdom he sang his songs.

No one else sang with such religious sentiment the grandeur of Zeus and the power of the gods of heaven as over against the demons of darkness.

He was most pious. Yet, despite all these considerations, being under the influence of the teachings of the sages and particularly of the Pythagorians, he dared to transform the myths, wherever this would help, into a kind of more noble apprehension of the nature of the gods.

PINDAR died in 448 at Argos* and following this there was a transfer of his relics to Thebes, the inhabitants of which, until the time of Pausanias (5th cen. B.C.), proudly displayed the tomb of their poet along with the ruins of his home, which was the ONLY exception Alexander the Great made in the general destruction of the city.

Pindar's muse sung of the gods, heroes and athletes, with victory hymns, laudations and lamentations.

Ancient grammarians collected his poetry into 17 books. Unfortunately, those that survived were only the victory hymns, small fragments of a dithyramb on the eclipse of the Sun in 463, two graceful songs for the priestesses of Corinth, the beautiful Theoxenos, and finally fragments of certain moving lamentations.

---

* A few words about this city will follow at the end of this section.

Some of his thoughts and views:

- Truth is Queen and an unshakable throne.
- Virtue that is praised grows like a tree.
- Experience shows us the virtue in which each one of us excels.
- When the happiness of a person is excessive, it doesn't last long.
- Law is the king of both the mortal and the immortal.
- All things are curable, so long as freedom isn't lost.
- Discover your possibilities and utilize them.
- The human being is a dream (an apparition).
- Custom is the king of all.
- No one on earth ever found a sign from the heavens regarding his or her future. For, the signs that foretell the future are past finding out for humans. There are many things that they don't expect and which happen against their desire, while, again, at other times terrible disasters are transformed in the shortest period of time into happy events.
- Old age is the childhood of eternity.
- Be a child with children, an adult with adults, an old person with old persons and adjust to all ages of life – that is the talent of the wise person.
- Time elusively hangs over a person.

ANAXAGORAS
(505-428 B.C.)

Anaxagoras was a famous sage of antiquity. He was born in 505 B.C. at Clazomenes (an ancient city of Ionia in Asia Minor) and died in 428 in Lampsako (an ancient city of the Hellespont).

Anaxagoras transferred philosophy from Ionia to Athens, where he established himself at about the middle of the 5th century B.C., in order to become a close friend of Pericles, of whom he also became teacher. However, on account of the theories that he articulated he was criticized for atheism by the opponents of the great politician and was forced to abandon Athens and to return to Ionia, where he established a philosophical school, probably at Lampsakos, where he also died occupying himself primarily with Mathematics, Physics, Astronomy etc.

He was the first to examine the issue squaring the circle and the first who formulated a monotheistic principle regarding the universe in which the Nous (Mind, Intellect) governs.

From his famous work "On Nature", unfortunately, few fragments has survived the sage correctly describes the phenomena of eclipses of the Moon.

Matter, according to Anaxagoras, is not changed into only one element. There are a multitude of elements, not only four, as Empedocles (philosopher of the 5th century B.C.) held.

He was the first to formulate the apprehension that the unformed and unmixed matter of the Universe was set into order by a "Mind" that created unity and harmony. The "Mind," he would say, is infinite, simple, and of a similar genus, and though the elements are completely passive, He has spontaneous energy, is free and self-determinate, the source of every life and movement. The elements do not possess self-consciousness, and the "Nous" knows all things, past, present, and future. He set and organized everything in its place purposefully. He is the eternal adorner of all things, the Autocrat.

In his cosmogonic theories he described stars, meteors, galaxies, and determined in a manner that was amazing for his time the causes that bring on the eclipses of the Sun (it is a piece of red lava because of its burning, he would say) and of the Moon (it has hills and gorges, he observed). Thus, he can be described as one who anticipated the theories of Byron, Kant, and Laplace and may be considered the forerunner of Comparative Physiology.

Some of his thoughts and views:

- All things were once together. Then came "Mind" that adorned everything.
- The descent into Hades is similar from all angles.

- Nous (mind) is the most delicate and most pure of all things.
- The aim of life is cognition and its emanation is freedom.
- The hand makes the person.
- Knowledge of visible things brings knowledge of invisible things.

PARMENIDES
(500-? B.C.)

Parmenides was a prominent philosopher of the Eleatic school. He lived and reached his high point around 500 B.C. and made laws for his fatherland of Elea (an ancient Greek city in Italy).

He was a friend of Xenophanes (an ancient Greek philosopher, 6th century B.C., founder of the Eleatic school) and of the Pythagorians.

Plato (428-347 B.C.) mentions that Parmenides came to Athens at the age of 65 years old and that Socrates (470-399 B.C.) who was then very young – he was 14-16 years old – associated with him. Thus we conclude that Parmenides must have been born in 520 B.C. and came to Athens around 455.

Parmenides, at the beginning of his career, was influenced by the theory of the Pythagorians, but later formed his own philosophical system.

The philosopher sharply censured the theory of Heraclitus (an ancient Greek philosopher, from Ephesus 544-480 B.C., founder of a significant philosophical school). However, he was unable to completely free himself from Ionic philosophy and Xenophanes's teaching. As much as he criticized the basic cosmogonic views (views and perspectives regarding the genesis, the creation of the cosmos) of the philosophers preceding him, he was not successful in setting forth his own solid, firm philosophical system which would controvert materialistic philosophy. To be sure, he introduced doubt and contradiction as basic elements of his critique of the ontological problem (a metaphysic having as its object nature, the essence of beings, the creation of the cosmos), yet he didn't pass over without prejudice into idealism (a philosophical orientation according to which the visible world is a product of imagination and only exists in cognition), because, as Aristotle (384-322 B.C.) informs us, he held many elements over from the philosophy of the Ionians. It was also for this reason that he accepted Earth and fire primarily as productive causes of material bodies.

Here we must mention that, in one of his dialogues with the same name, Plato expresses exceptional admiration for Parmenides, while on the contrary, Aristotle combated the theories of Parmenides and the whole Eleatic school.

On Nature is the only work of Parmenides that is mentioned.

In this great and instructive poem which was written in hexameter verses and in the Ionian dialect, he immortalized his teaching which possessed a peculiar dyadic character, since it accepts the simultaneous existence of a single aetherial fire and an unillumined darkness.

The work of the philosopher, of which only fragments have survived, was praised by critics of ancient art because besides the fact that it presented his significant philosophy, it was also a marvelous poetic creation.

Finally, regarding his teaching, which was supported on the theory of the spherical nature of the Earth and its zones, it has been proved that it possesses great significance for the scientific study of human beings.

Some of his thoughts and views:

- Let the criterion be reason, because the senses lead astray.
- In the present exists the unique, singular and undivided.
- The eternity of the being derives "absolutely" from its necessity, thus: "What is born derives from what is similar to it, but the dissimilar has no reason to be born from the similar or to produce the similar; if, on the contrary, the dissimilar was born from the similar, Being would derive from non-Being."
- Human beings were first born from the Sun.
- One is the aim of the whole universe: to name the Being.
- To cognize and to exist. It's one and the same.
- The Being is, has reality; the Non-Being is not, has not reality. (Being exists; non-being does not exist).
- Since no separate being absolutely possesses "Beinghood" it can never be identified with that beinghood.
- The central core of the cosmos, or Earth, consists of fire, and fire, moreover, constitutes the external crown or wall (that is, heaven).

PHILOLAOS

(5th Century B.C.)

Philolaos was a pythagorian philosopher. He was born around the middle of the 5th century B.C. at Krotona* of Italy, where he became initiated into Pythagorianism, probably by Lysis. He lived and taught many years at Thebes, contributing decisively in the dissemination of Pythagorianism in Greece.

His students, who possessed noteworthy spiritual development and activity, were Simmias and Kebes. They are mentioned in Plato's *Phaedo* as holding converse with Socrates.

According to his theory:

- All things are done, or "become," by necessity and harmony.
- The principles of all things is the FINITE (Contingent), the INFINITE and the ARITHMITICAL MONAD, which, when it is added to the infinite creates the finite and when added to the finite creates the infinite.
- The Earth is at the center of the Universe among other planets that revolve around a "Central fire."

  Before his death he returned to Italy where he also died, unknown when.

  Of his works only fragments have survived, whose authenticity, however, is doubted.

  At all events, the views contained in these works are recognized to be characteristic of the Pythagorian School at the time of Philolaos.

Some of his thoughts and views:

- The harmony of things and of the world is a synthesis of the fundamental antithesis of the INFINITE and the FINITE.
- Synthesis is a work of number which is not identified with the beings (or realities), but is something that beings possess and by which they become known.
- Number, or quantity, is suitable to entities pertaining to the soul and its harmony extends as power from divinized things to human works (art, music, medicine, etc.)
- The essence of beings is related to the monad that contracts within it the finite and the infinite.

* A city of southern Italy, which was established by the Achaians of the Peloponese in 7 B.C.

- Ten is the most perfect number.
- Ten is the fundamental antithesis; ten are the heavenly bodies that revolve around the Focal Point of everything.
- The soul is the harmony of the body which is maintained even after death.

PROTAGORAS

(5th century b.C.)

Protagoras was a famous sophist. He was born in 480 B.C. at Abdera (an ancient city of Thrace). He was a contemporary of Socrates and his initial profession was that of a porter.

Democritus discovered him, took him beside him and made him his secretary and student.

He went about various Greek cities, as well as in Southern Italy, teaching the art of Rhetoric.

When he went to Athens he became closely associated with Pericles and Euripides and was particularly honored by the Athenians.

Protagoras, like Heraclitus, believed in the constant flow of beings in the Universe. Human beings, he used to say, know things not as they are, but as they appear to their senses. Every item of knowledge is subjective and items of knowledge that are generated from the senses and nature differ in each individual in proportion to the difference of the organs that receive the external presentations. In other words, everything is exactly how to appears to the individual. According to Protagoras, therefore, there are no truths that are valid. Thus, something which to one person appears true, can appear false to another. For each thing, he taught, there are two contrary views. He considered virtue simply as a good habit that prepares a better psychical disposition and admonishes people toward right action.

For the existence of the gods, Protagoras would say: "I know nothing, because two things obstruct me: the darkness of the matter and the brevity of human life."

On these thoughts Schiller rightly observes: "For his time, these discussions were provocative to the extreme. An open battle against all accepted ideas of the epoch was the result, and yet, they were formulated in a double-slicing style with classical tranquility."

For the above theories, Protagoras, as it was natural for his time, was criticized for atheism and his books were burnt publicly at the market place. After this, his friends escaped in the night. On his way to Sicily he drowned in the ocean at the age of about 70.

His most important work was "On truth" or as it is otherwise called "Establishing truths" (studies that topple all chain to knowledge).

Some of his thoughts and views:

- Man is the measure of all things, of the beings (or realities) as they are, and of the non-beings as they are not.

- Nothing exists. But if it does exist, it is incomprehensible to man; but even if it does become comprehensible, it cannot be explained to the neighbor.
- Everyone judges things with the measure of one's rational faculty or power. Whatever appears right, this is also really right. This judgment is right until the day some other person proves the opposite with logical proofs.

STOBAIOS
(5th century B.C.)

- The egoist gathers together the world to himself; the altruist gives himself to the whole world.
- There is a form of modesty that is nothing but the cloak of pride.
- Prudence is a very difficult thing for the rich person.
- Flexibility is a grace for the body, virtue for the spirit, but a fault for the conscience.

MELISSOS
(5th century B.C.)

A philosopher from Samos, a politician and admiral, who peaked in the middle of the 5th century. B.C. In 441 B.C. he supported the autonomy of his fatherland – the time of rebellion – according to the expansionist policy of Athens and defeated the general Pericles (490-429 B.C.) in a naval battle.

Melissos, who supported the ideas of the Eleatic philosophical school, belongs with Zeno the Eleatic (490-430 B.C.), to the third generation of Eleatic philosophers, after Xenophanes (6th cen. B.C.) and Parmenides (6th cen. B.C.), of whom he was a student. In his work "On Nature or On Being" Melissos occupied himself with the broader exposition and analysis of the views and theories of the first Eleatics and with repelling the polemics of Empedocles (5th cen. B.C.).

The philosopher taught that the understanding of the being constitutes the object of the rational process, while he tried to prove the non-existence of movement, by contending that there is no void. The Dialectic (a method of conversation with questions and answers utilized to discover truth) of Melissos offered many services to the attempt of understanding the essence of beings and led to the skepticism of the sophists.

Some of his thoughts and views:

- The Being is unchanging, there is no void, because the void is nothing (!) and consequently neither does movement exist, because movement undermines the void.
- If this Being is complete, it remains unmoved; being divided it moves; but in moving, it cannot be being.
- That which is, was and always will be.
- If it is infinite, it is one.

SOPHOCLES
(496-406 B.C.)

The Second of the three (Aeschylus, Sophocles, Euripides) greatest tragic poets of the 5th century B.C. and one of the most prominent poets the world has known. He was born in the attic deme of Colonos at 496 B.C., where he also died at the age of 90, that is, in 406 B.C.

His parents were wealthy and for this reason he was given the opportunity to become cultivated and well educated, and being the charismatic youth that he was, from a child he came in first in gymnastics and musical contests.

His musical education was so great that he composed the chorals of his tragedies himself.

He was taught tragedy by the great teacher of tragic poetry, Aeschylus, whom indeed he defeated with his first appearance as a dramatic poet, in the contest in 468, with the tetralogy "Troptolemos." Judges of the contest were the ruler of Athens Kimon (an Athenian politician and general 510-449 B.C.) and his co-generals whom he compelled to sit in theater and to judge.

For ten whole years these great tragedians dominated the theater with alternating first place victories.

It is said that he competed with Euripides for the first time in 438, whom he also defeated.

Sophocles was an uneasy and restless man. For this reason he became interested also in the political issues of the city of Athens, whose inhabitants honored him and indeed after his presentation of *Antigone* they chose him general in the war against the Samians (441-439).

In that time he became Herodotus's friend, whose historical work he also studied.

Our poet was friend of the Athenian people and, being the free thinker that he was, he never appeared in the court of the tyrant or king, like Aeschylus, Euripides, Agathon (a Greek tragedian of the 5th century B.C.) and others.

In his personal life, Sophocles was affable, gracious and a friend of eros.

He died in deep old age during the fall of the year 406 and was buried in his paternal tomb which was on the road to Dekeleia (Tatoi), and on his tomb there was set a siren.

In order to especially honor the virtuous, great poet, the deme ordained, by vote, for a sacrifice to be offered him each year.

Finally, by the proposal of the rhetorician, Lycurgus, a great statue was set up at the theater of Dionysius, a copy of which is a marble statue that he found in the museum of Laterano in Rome.

According to Aristophanes, Sophocles wrote 123 dramas, and even some elegies and victory songs.

It is characteristic that during the dramatic contests that would usually take place at that time, during the feasts of Dionysius, Sophocles won more victories than Aeschylus and Euripides. It is calculated that he came in first place 18-20 times and many times second place. But never third place.

What has survived of his great work are fragments from certain satirical dramas, as well as fragments of other dramas and only seven tragedies, as listed below:

1. AIAS. Perhaps the most ancient of surviving dramas of the poet.

   SUBJECT: After the death of Achilles, a judgment (evaluation) took place regarding who wouldl take his weapons. And because Odysseus was preferred, Aias was taken over by mania (madness, insanity) and maniacally attacked the herds of Achaians, where he slaughters animals and shepherds, thinking that he's attacking his enemies etc.

2. ANTIGONE, one of the most beautiful dramas of Sophocles most probably performed in the year 442 and resulted, as we previously mentioned, in his being elected general in the war against the Samians.

   SUBJECT: Creon, king of Thebes, publicly made known his command for the body of Polyneiki to remain unburied (son of Oedipus), because he militated against his fatherland together with foreign kings (rulers) and simultaneously, the order stated that, if someone buries him, he will be punished by death.

   Fraternal love, however, overcame human orders and laws. Thus we see Antigone, after the dialogue that she had with her sister Ismene, who tried to dissuade her from not following the commands of Creon (an uncle who abandoned the kingdom, after the death of Oedipus's sons, Eteocli and Polyneiki) and to come into conflict with the authorities. Despite all these things Antigone later confesses that she buried her brother because she didn't want to transgress the "unwritten divine laws" and she earns the known price of the commandment, etc.

3. ELECTRA, who continually laments her murdered father and yearns for the punisher (vindicator) Orestes; and her sister Chrysothemis doesn't oppose her etc...

4. OEDIPUS TYRANNOS, an amazing tragedy of fate and of tragic irony. It was written at the beginning of the Peloponesean War (spring of 431 B.C.).

SUBJECT: According to mythology, Oedipus (a mythical king of Thebes) took for wife his mother, IOKASTE and when, after many years, he discovered the fact he blinded himself, etc.

5. THE WOMEN OF TRACHIS, the weakest of the surviving dramas of the poet,
which took the name from the chorus that consisted of the women of Trachinos.

6. PHILOCTETES, was performed 409 B.C. and took first prize.

SUBJECT: Philoktetes, when he was bitten by a snake, was abandoned by the Achaians at the island of Lemnos. However, because, according to an oracle, Troy was about to be dominated by the arrows of Hercules, which Philoktetes had, Odysseus went to Lemnos with Neoptolemus, son of Achilles, in order to take the arrows, etc.

7. OEDIPUS AT COLONUS: The time of the instruction, the performance, is not certain. It is said that it took place at about 401.

SUBJECT: Oedipus, in deep old age, leaves his fatherland and being guided by the hand of his daughter Antigone, comes into Athens, according to the oracle, in order to die at Colonus, the birthplace of Sophocles, etc.

Some of his thoughts and views:

- There are many things that are fearful, but nothing is more fearful than man.
- You're miserable because you mockingly laugh at me; tomorrow they will mockingly laugh at you, too.
- The mistake is not an unusual thing for human beings and whoever makes mistakes, is neither worthy of condemnation, nor unforgivable, if one isn't indifferent about one's fault and indeed when one tries as much as possible to correct it.
- There is no wilder animal than the human being when his or her impulse is as equally powerful as his or her passion.
- The same thing happens to all people; we only think of our own self.

- For the just person to become visible, time is needed, while the unjust person appears in a single day.
- It is better for one to keep silent than to say unworthy, worthless words.
- Create peace with your neighbor and declare war against your faults.
- Quarrels, insults, birth the tyrant.
- Envy pursues the one who possesses riches, fame, virtue and happiness.
- Whatever might be the achievements of a person in the future, he or she won't find a way to avoid death.
- You can be sure that a nation in which impudence and tax immunity remain unpunished, will find, after a pleasant trip, a plunge into the abyss.
- The lie never lives so long as for it to grow old.
- Each thing is good in its proper time.
- Whatever one seeks out one finds; whatever one neglects one loses.
- The cosmetic adornment of a woman is silence.
- Only time will reveal the just man.
- Old age is painful, not because delights cease, but because we stop hoping.
- Wherever you search, you will find pain.
- There is no greater evil than anarchy.
- No one loves life so much as the old person.
- I was not born to hate, but to love.
- No worse thing has ever appeared among human beings than money.
- Obstinacy is paid with reversals.
- Those who hurry too much trip.

EMPEDOCLES
(495-435 B.C.)

Empedocles was a great philosopher from Acraganta of Sicily, who peaked around 450 B.C. It is said that he fell into the disfavor of the deme and was forced to leave, in advanced age for the Peloponese, where he also died.

The fate of Empedocles is among the most eccentric.

A great poet, thinker, a distinguished doctor (Calien attributes to him the founding of the "Italian School" of Medicine), a reformer, a pioneer of democracy (1870 the Sicilians set him side by side with Garibaldi!), an engineer, a physicist, he embraced with enthusiasm Pythagoras's theory of metempsychosis, and in dying left behind the image of a philosopher.

He was the son of the ruler Metona, and with the death of his father (444 B.C.), he denied the royal crown, which they offered him, out of respect for the equality of the citizens. And occupying himself successfully in the political matters of his fatherland, he established a democratic state in Acraganta.

His contemporaries worshipped him and particularly honored him as a very intelligent man. Thus, the significant city of Acraganta, which believed in the divine origin of Empedocles, set up for him a grandiose temple and a brilliant statue.

Empedocles accepts, like Anaxagoras and Heraclitus, the derivation of the beings through evolution and thus may be regarded as the forerunner of the Darwinian Theory. He studied the phenomenon of the Universe and Nature and the views that he formulated don't differ much from those of modern Physics and Astronomical Science.

It is said that Empedocles wrote many works on Politics, Medicine, History and metered verses.

His primary work measuring 5000 verses was distributed in two great poems "On Nature" and "Purifications," in which, with a special, characteristic manner, he develops his theories regarding the creation of the Universe and the descent of beings and various moral theories.

- The first book, "On Nature," consists of three books:

The first treats of the general canons, or rules, of BEING and the theory of EVERYTHING.

The second is the particular promotion and advancement of the BEINGS (or REALITIES) and

The third deals with the formation of the human being and indeed of the soul.

- His second poem "Purifications" consists of an extensive book, in which various moral theories and thoughts are mentioned.

Unfortunately, of his complete works only a few hundred verses of each work survive.

Between the ancient and modern world there is a difference of ooinion as regards the classification of Empedocles.

Thus, the ancients classify him among the Pythagorians, and the more modern thinkers with Heraclitus.

Some of his thoughts and views:

- It is difficult to find a wise person, because to do so, you have to be wise yourself.
- I left God and roam aimlessly on earth.
- It isn't difficult to change nature.
- The Arcragantinoi party as if they're going to die tomorrow and build houses like they're about to live eternally.
- Happy is the person who has acquired the wealth of divine thoughts, and unfortunate is the one who possesses a dark idea regarding the gods.
- Nature is not the work of anyone, but is a mixture and harmony of many elements.

ZENON
(490-430 B.C.)

Zeno was an Eleatic, a Greek philosopher of the Eleatic School. He was born in the ancient Greek city of Elea of Italy in 490 B.C., where he lived and died in 430.

He was a student of Parmenides (Eleatic philosopher of the 6th century B.C.) who battled against all the theories of those who accepted the notion that Being does not exist, but that many things exist and everywhere there exists movement and change. He is the first "logos-contender" or "word-warrior" who denied movement, proving the possibility of acceleration. According to Zeno, each movement is only phenomenal, or as we would more usually say, apparent, because the laws of movement are found to be in contradiction with the nature of things. Moreover, he taught with fanaticism that movement cannot be finished and that every movement is relative. Beyond his theories, Zeno succeeded in becoming known to Greek antiquity because he created the basis of "formal logic" which was supported exclusively by pure cognition. Zenon, we may say, is the first who used the syllogism of "Reductio ad absurdum" or "impossible reduction." For this reason, but also for his significant but contradictory theories, Aristotle named him "founder of Dialectic."

Aristotle, who studied the theories of Zeno, informs us that Zeno denies movement.

On this matter the philosopher Hegel, who cannot be considered a suspicious anti-aristotelian systematician, says:

> "Aristotle writes that Zeno denies movement, because it contains within it an internal contradiction. Yet, this must not be interpreted as a denial of its existence. It never crossed the mind of Zeno to deny its existence. That which he is looking to comprehend is its truth; and for Zenon movement is non-true, because it is contradictory."

It is said that Zeno, by command of the tyrant Eleas Nearchus, was condemned to a martyris death and was pounded in mortar, after analogous dreadful tortures, and this, because the sage worked to free the Eleatics from the tyranny of Nearchus.

Some of his thoughts and views:

- As an answer to the pressing question: "Does anything in truth exist that is unmoved?" Zenon says: "Why yes! The dart in its flight is unmoved."

- The one who says depraved things differs from the one doing depraved things only as regards the lack of opportunity.
- The world is so small that it could fit in the hand of a single honorable human being.
- The will of parents is to have primacy in honors.
- It is not good for one to speak right things; it is good for the speaker to do the things that he says.

NIKIAS
(469-413 B.C.)

- The egoist seeks solitude in order to avoid subjection.
- All of us complain of the brevity of life, and yet, how much time do we waste.

KRATES
(450 B.C.)

- Time brought me down. Time, which is a wise architect, with its work, makes everything become weak and sick.
- I try to hold the reigns of my stomach, and whoever doesn't know how to hold them, can expect many evils.
- Both for the old and the young person, it is a valuable thing to hold their tongue in silence.

EURIPIDES
(485-407 B.C.)

Euripides was one of the three great tragic poets of ancient Greece. According to the information that prevailed, he was born in 480 B.C. at Salamina the same day that Xerxes' fleet was routed. More probably, however, it appears that he was born in 485-484. Things aren't all that clear with regard to his descent. Thus, many of the ancients held the view that Euripides did not descend from an aristocratic family (his mother sold vegetables), but other sources prove that his origin was most noble, just as that of his two other dramatic companions, Aeschylus and Sophocles.

Euripides acquired a very fine education, which was also proved by the products of his intellect.

As a youth he occupied himself with sports and particularly with wrestling and boxing, which, however, he quickly abandoned in order to occupy himself with spiritual works.

His great love for Philosophy pushed him to study the writings of the earlier philosophers and to follow the teachings of his contemporaries, Anaxagoras, Prodicus and Protagoras. He was a student and friend of Socrates to such a degree that it was rumored by many that the philosopher worked with him in the writing of the tragedies.

It was natural that these associations influenced not only his character, but also the great development and cultivation of his intellect.

Euripides abstained from active politics, but was attentive and closely followed the important political issues and had great zeal in teaching his wholesome political theories, which the ruling mob rejected. He, however, set himself against oligarchy and its representatives and preferred the middle class citizens to prevail, whom he considered saviors of the city and stable friends of order and orderliness. Here we must mention that, having become disgusted by Athenian Imperialism, which was preparing, after the destruction of Melos (416), to conquer Syracuse and Sicily, he wrote the most violent accusation in antiquity against the war in "Trojan Women."

However, characteristic features of Euripides are that he was pious, passionately loved his fatherland, and didn't spare any opportunity to castigate the enemies of his fatherland. According to tradition, Euripides was morose, pensive and rarely did anyone see him smiling. That is, he had the strict countenance of the most sophisticated moralist, rather than the creative cheerfulness of the God-inspired poet.

The last years of his life he passed in the court of the King of Macedonia Archelaos (5th – 4th century B.C.), whom, in order to honor him, be wrote the tragedy "Archelaos," in which he praises King Heracledi as being the founder of the Macedonian Dynasty.

The great tragedian died in Macedonia where he was also buried in the fall of 407.

Later, by Lycurgus' proposal, the bronze statue of Dionysus was set up at the Dionysian theater.

Euripides, besides a victory song, which he wrote for Alcibiades (448-404 B.C.), when he had won in the chariot-races, and one elegy for the Athenians who fell at Syracuse, in that destructive campaign (415-413 B.C.), wrote 92 dramas (23 tetralogies). Of these only 19 have survived, among which was also a satire, the "Cyclops" (Medea, Hippolitus, Phoenissae, Iphegenia in Aulis, Alcestis, Andromache, Bacchae, Hecuba, Helen, Electra, Heracleides, Heracles, Suppliants, Ion, Cyclops, Orestis, Trojan Women, Rhesos) and very few tetralogies.

Euripides was a modernist and for this reason he often provoked the reservations of established citizens, of judges and generally of all conservative people. This resulted in the conservative judges, who would judge the dramatical plays that were done at that time during the festivals of Dionysus (Bacchus=the God of earth fertility, of wine, and of the vineyard of the ancient Greeks), not liking his works. So, although for the first time he took part in the contests in 455 (he received third prize), in 441, that is, at the age of 39, he barely succeeded taking first prize. Finally, he had only 5 first place victories. However, as much as Euripides didn't like the conservatives, that much more did he like the youth, who worshipped him and would call him most wise.

Comparison to the great tragedians:

AESCHYLUS is the most austere tragedian who in his works represents the brave, prideful and pious mind-set and mentality of the generation of Marathon fighters and praises the liberators of Greece. He presents people "better than what they are."

SOPHOCLES is the praiser of heroes, who presents Pericles' generation, in which prevailed in all things measure and harmony and depicts people "as they should be."

EURIPIDES, the interpreter of human passions, who in his tragedies depicts the turmoils of the contemporary generation, was influenced by the spirit of the sophists and scientific research pertaining to divine and human things. He presents human beings "as they are."

Some of his thoughts and views:

- Who knows if life is death and death life?
- Hopes nourish the down-trodden.

- You won't be able to prosper without labor; it is shameful not to want to work hard.
- Whoever has neglected learning during their youth, has lost irreplaceable time and has killed the future.
- Virtue comes by hard work.
- Three are the virtues that you ought to inculcate in your child: to honor the gods, the parents who brought you up, and the laws of Greece. And if you do these things, you will always have the best crown of glory.
- Second thoughts are better.

PERICLES
(490-429 B.C.)

The man that gave his name to a century – the golden period not only of Athens, but also of Greek art and of Greek civilization – he was born around 490 B.C. from an aristocratic Athenian family.

At a very young age he learned by being close to the most famous men of his time: Zeno the Eleatic, the musician Damona, the philosopher Anaxagoras (who first formulated the monotheistic concept for the Universe, which Mind governs), from whom he acquired an enlightened education, which later would appear in his political philosophy and which would leave an inelible seal in the Athens of Pericles.

Even though he was an aristocrat by descent, Pericles in 469 is found at the head of the democratic party and begins his political career, being an opponent of another gifted man, Kimon (a politician and general 510-449 B.C.) who was the leader of aristocrats.

After the death of Ephialte PERICLES then received a governing position in the Athenian commonwealth.

He served as a general and an exemplary governor and rhetorician who knew how to seize and take prisoner the multitude by his speech. Thucydides, who was a great admirer of his, gives us an example of his charming speech in the "Funeral Oration of Pericles," where, among other things, he informs us about the visions and thoughts of the politician.

In his days, and since the glorious or unfortunate wars (Corinth-Aegina- Megara- Sparta, Medean wars etc.) the city was rebuilt and the army and administration were reorganized.

In 446, one important episode occurred in his political carrer history, during which he restored the eternal conflict existing between Sparta and Athens, which held up for an entire 15 years.

The many years of truce allowed Pericles to adorn the city with new beautiful and grandiose buildings. Thus he created a new Athens, his own personal masterpiece. And with a daring architectural plan, he made the Acropolis a real adornment of Athens, which, with the unwaning light of the Parthenon, continues to illumine the peoples throughout the ages, with the immortal ancient Greek spirit.

The above gave to the city with an immortal magnificence and made the name of Pericles one of the most famous of all time.

By means of his domestic politics he put into effect many democratic and socio-political reforms. Now, in wanting to strengthen the spiritual, moral, and musical education of the people, he implemented a special reward for citizens for their services toward the state, he established education free of charge for the poor, as well as their free entrance to the theaters (the poor citizens would receive money from the public treasury – the theoretical – for the payment of the theatrical ticket) and he granted to the citizens of the lowest classes the right to be able to rise up to power. Finally, the Athenian trade developed very much and expanded from East to West.

PERICLES gathered within himself a rare cultivation and a great aestheticism, as his works and his friendship with top artists, poets and philosophers (Pheidias- Sophocles-Anaxagoras) prove, as well as his connection with the super-cultivated and most beautiful Aspasia - the feminist of the time.

Incorruptible in public life, "he didn't increase the price of his paternal property even a single drachma." He expected the same innocence also from the others, not only in Government, but of those of his house too.

Though unimpeachable as a "public figure," in his private life, on the contrary, he provoked scandals which weakened his influence on the people. Especially sensitive to the charm of women, Pericles, as Thucydides informs us, "risked danger in his career because of a courtesan."

On account of his peaceful character, his exquisite rhetorical virtues and the true divine wealth of monuments that he raised up in Athens, they likened him to Zeus, who granted to the city of Athens an entire "Golden Age."

He died in 429, after he had lived through the most dreadful starvation and had seen each one of his sons die one by one. To someone who had sat down at his death bed and was formulating the laudation of his virtues and his works, he observed that he had forgotten his great unique value, namely that he owed nothing to chance: "No Athenian," he said, "wore on account of me a black mantle of pain."

The sculptor Crysilas created an idealistic statue or Pericles out of bronze, copies of which are to be found in the museum of the Vatican, at the Museaum of Berlin and in the British Museum.

Some of his thoughts and views:

- All the earth is a grave for famous men.
- Time is the best advisor.
- I believe that, if a city in its whole is found to be at its acme, it serves the citizens much better, than in the case where each of its citizens prospers, but the state in its totality is suffering misfortune.
- Every citizen has the right to education and aesthetic delight.
- When you lighten the burdens on the citizen, he becomes stronger for the fatherland and his hands become more eagerly willing for work.
- The great honors for the citizen derive from dangers that he will suffer for the sake of the fatherland.
- The person who dies is incapable of being envied.

ASPASIA
(522-423 B.C.)
A SUCCESSFUL FEMINIST?

Aspasia, the "shameless courtesan" of Pericles, as the comedian Kratinos (522-423 B.C.) describes her, is the symbol of the attempt for the emancipation of women in ancient Greece.

An emancipation simultaneously sexual and intellectual. She truly belongs to the limited group of high class "courtesans" who accompany the more famous men of the time – politicians, artists, people of letters – and are famous not only for their rare beauty, but also for their grace and cleverness of mind. They had the same freedom as men, the same political and cultural interests. Naturally, they paid for this freedom with "esteem" and they escaped not only the scornful names (they called her Hera, because of her relationship with Olympian Pericles), but also the most degrading adjectives.

Aspasia was born in Miletus (an ancient city of Ionia) and came in 450, in the prime of life, to Athens, where she opened a school of rhetoric and philosophy. Her lessons were attended, not only by girls of good families and young ladies accompanied by their husbands, but also by many people of like spirit, like Socrates, Anaxagoras, Phedias and Pericles himself. The great politician fell in love with the courtesan and took her to live together with him, abandoning his wife (445 B.C.), with whom he had been in disagreement for a sufficiently good amount of time.

With Aspasia the home of Pericles was transformed into a kind of literary parlor, like the ones that existed in France, during the time of the Enlightenment, open to all kinds of discussions. Aspasia became the "first lady" of Athens: she not only regulated fashion but she also represents Athenian delicacy in the most brilliant way.

This situation, however, created envy and in parallel course gave opportunities for Pericles' opponents, which resulted in the making of a scandal. Pericles was accused of having turned his house into a "place of perdition," and that "he was enjoying entertainment with girls whom Aspasia, the pimp, was purchasing." But not even his friends escaped slander. Phedias was jailed for theft and for sacrilege. Anaxagoras was sent into exile. Aspasia was dragged to court with the charge of "impiety" towards the gods and Greece. At her trial, which took place before 500 judges, Pericles defended her. It was a gripping defence, because Pericles not only summoned all his excellent rhetorical powers, but he was even moved during his delivery to such a degree, that he was seen crying. This sight so touched the judges, that Aspasia was absolved despite the pressures that had been exerted. But the popularity of Pericles had toppled irreparably. His death, three years later, ended an uncontrolled decline.

GORGIAS
(483-375 B.C.)

Gorgias was born at Leontinus of Italy (Sicily) in 483 B.C. and died in 375 B.C.

Gorgias was a student of Empedocles (5th cen. B.C.) and was famous for his powerful rhetorical capabilities and his learning. Seeing, perhaps dimly, the need of a global, universal language of civilization, he adopted for this purpose the attic dialect.

Before the first Sicilian campaign of the Athenians (spring of 415 B.C.), the famous and powerful orator visited Athens.

Together with the one sent from Sicily, that is, Gorgias, "The New teaching", SOPHISM (the Art of the sophists), made its first official appearance, which was a important factor for the cultivation of a new type of man in Greece. It brought on a significant change in Greek life and its influence became clear in all branches of social activity, particularly in politics.

In 392 B.C., the elder Gorgias had delivered in Olympia before those gathered for the national Olympic celebration of the Greeks, an impetuous and flaming speech against the Persians, and it recommended to the Panhellenes to stop their internal wars and to become reconciled, to restore their broken friendly relations (to be of the same mind).

Gorgias wrote many works, but they were all lost. According to his teaching, the philosopher does not look to seek out the truth, because the truth objectively doesn't exist (so the sophists believed); but looks to educate people for a purposeful, beneficial and pleasant life.

Some of his thoughts and views:

- "Neither the non-Being exists, nor the Being."
- If the Being exists or can become known, it is not capable of being transmitted with words."
- What is true is whatever is to the interest of the individual, and what is good is whatever benefits.

THUCYDIDES
(470-396 B.C.)

Chronologically speaking, Thucydides is the first critical historiographer and noteworthy attic prose-writer.

He was born at the ancient deme of Alimounta (today's Alimo) in 470 B.C. and died in Scapti Hyli in 396 B.C.

He belonged to the wealthiest and most aristocratic class of Attica and this resulted in his receiving a most thorough and wholesome education and upbringing. As teachers he had the philosopher Anaxagoras (505-428 B.C.) and the rhetorician Antiphonta who in his writings praises virtue. Besides these, those who had an influence in the formation of Thucydides' character, his ethos, his language, his spirituality and in general, his overall cultural make-up, were Gorgias (a sophist and rhetorician, died in 388 B.C) and Prodicus of Ceos, as well as other sages, who gathered together in Athens, which constituted the spiritual center of the Nation.

In 424 B.C. he was named general of the campaign that took place in the regions of Thasos and of Thrace, where he was known and exercised great influence, because in the region of Thrace (Scapte Hyli) he had rights to use the gold mine that was located there. However, because this campaign failed and Brasidas (a Spartan general) at Amphipoli (a colony of Athens which is at the shores of the river Strymona), which he was unable to save, he was accused of betrayal and was condemned to death. But he escaped execution because he expatriated in time and exiled himself for twenty years, which he spent at his estates in Thrace, but also in traveling.

This departure of his benefited the history of letters, because the exiled Thucydides found the time to travel about places that had become a theatre of war, and he studied the events completely without distraction. It appears that he must have visited Italy and Sicily, as the clear narration of military events in Sicily indicates, during that unfortunate Athenian campaign. He remained for a short while with the philomuse King Archelao of Macedonia (5th – 4th century B.C.).

In 404 B.C., Thucydides returned to Athens and after a short chronological time he returned to his estates in Thrace (Scapti Hyli), where in all probability he began to write his History.

According to legend, he was murdered in 396 B.C. The sudden death of Thucydides became the reason why his work was not completed, which he began to write, day by day, from the beginning, with scholastic precision and impartiality (he stops suddenly at the victory of the Athenians at Kynos during a point of mutilation at the Hellespont – in the middle of our September of 411 B.C., that is, in the twenty first year of the Peloponnesian war 431-404 B.C.)

Thucydides was an objective, trustworthy, modest and moral man. His blameless life and the strictness of his appearance were clearly visible in the characteristic features of his face.

If in Herodotus (an ancient Greek historian 484-410 B.C.) History becomes a narration – a chronical and myth combined – in Thucydides it is the search for truth, a scientific method. History is no longer the personality, but the event. It is the critical research of causes, of evolutions, and of consequences. With Thucydides, who doesn't reject the duty of criticism, and who from different views suggests what is most trustworthy, with absolute impartiality, and without passion or malice, history truly becomes the guide of life. After all, how could it be otherwise, since it is a work of people who create with their spirit and their will!

Thucydides himself would say: "I wrote my History in order for it to be an immortal asset to people and not as a work of transient competition, that is, for a time-band audience."

As a critical historian he attributes the causes of whatever things have occurred in the world, as well as the painful consequences of the war, not to the gods, as Herodotus did, but to natural causes and to human nature which regulate all things, having as protagonists the passions, greed, vain glory, etc. For this reason, in describing the mania of the civil wars, he condemns their motivating factors. Here we can say that Thucydides recognizes the chasm existing between politics and morality and thus he becomes the great forerunner of Machiavelli (an Italian politician and historian 1469-1527).

During the civil wars, when hatred, slaughter, destruction, fear and wrath took on monstrous dimensions (the Peloponnesian war), Thucydides stands above the wild passions, and sees things with a clear mind, with a calm and measured tone, placing above the fatherland freedom and goals, the TRUTH AND ONLY THE TRUTH.

By way of concluding we can say that the book of Thucydides is marvelous for its leanness, clarity, and objectivity, and as PLUTARCH (an ancient Greek Biographer 46-127 A. D.) writes, "the readers become spectators of the events." The best example of this testimony is the narration of the starvation of Athens, a shockingly terrible image of the despair of death...

Finally, with regard to Thucydides' book, Hegel (a German philosopher 1770-1831) would say: "The only unique profit that accrued to humanity from the Peloponnesian war is the history of Thucydides."

Some of his thoughts and views:

- Such is the indifference of the many, who don't labor in order to accurately examine the truth but prefer ready formulations.

- According to the tradition of our fathers, virtues are acquired by means of labor.
- You will be persuaded by your own life experience that very few things are achieved with tempestuous desire, while most things are achieved with calm and prudent foresight.
- So strange is the nature of human beings that they disdain the ones who flatter them and greatly admire the ones who don't subject themselves to discipline.
- Lack of learning brings on impudence; of thought brings on laziness.
- We all have a tendency towards sin, either as individuals or as groups, and there is no law to obstruct us, since people have tasted all the forms of punishment without any positive result and they even reached surpassing strictness with the hope of anticipating more effectively the crimes of evil-doers.
- Vindication doesn't always follow the injustice a person has suffered, nor is strength a sure thing, because it is full of hopes. The scale of chance is so unstable that we cannot support ourselves much upon it. Yet, it gives us valuable lessons.
- Fear adversely impacts even the memory.
- The sufferings that you will undergo shall become your lessons.
- It is not a shameful thing to be poor; doing shameful things is shameful.
- We must endure with fortitude and without murmuring the blows that the gods deal us, but we must deal courageously against the blows of our enemies.
- That which you are contemplating on doing, do it right away and without delays.
- Chance helps those who dare.
- History is an eternal work, not a Rhetorical exercise to be heard at a contest.
- The best way and the surest defense for the army is for it to preserve its strict discipline and to obey its officers.
- The most usual consequence of the unforeseen and sudden prosperity of a people is for its citizens to become vainglorious and arrogant. On the contrary, the good things that were acquired with prudence are more stable and certain and are maintained more than those things that chance brings. In a word, people are more capable of repelling misfortune than of keeping their prosperity.

SOCRATES
(470-399 B.C.)

Socrates was one of the wisest men of antiquity. He was born in 470 B.C. at Athens, died there in 399 B.C., after having drunk the hemlock.

As all middle Athenian citizens, Socrates too, at the age of 18 years old, was entered into the military registry. He was placed in the army as a hoplite, that is, the heavy infantry which constituted the foundational strength of the Greek army. During the Peloponnesian war (431-405 B.C.) he fulfilled his duty towards the fatherland and struggled with great courage and fortitude at Potidaea, where he saved the life and weapons of the young Alcibiades (432), at Delium (424) and at Amphipolis (422).

He lived and taught in an epoch during which political, social and moral institutions were tangibly losing their strength and were toppling. Thus with his teaching he was accused of introducing "new demons" and "corrupting the young."

He was relatively poor and in his youth he had learned sculpting at his father's workshop. Having a powerful, restless and pure intellect, he attended the lessons of many philosophers of his time. Initially he was influenced by the teaching of Anaxagoras and of Archelaos. Later he turned to the sophists like Protagoras, and Gorgias, etc., and having formed his own apprehensions he began to teach and to develop his own theories, which distinguished him as the greatest philosopher of all ages.

Socrates had as object, or as we usually say in English, the subject-matter of his research, the HUMAN BEING, in comparison to the ancient Greek thinkers who had as the center of their study the physical world, nature, the Universe (namely *the Pre-socratics*: Philosophers of the 7th until the 5th century B.C. who were physicists, astronomers, mathematics, like Thales, Anaximander, Heraclitus, Pythagoras, Empedocles, Anaxagoras etc.) Justly Cicero would say: "Socrates brought philosophy from heaven down to earth." Thus we see his study taking interest only in truth, virtue, knowledge and in the urging of human beings to search their inner, esoteric world and their environment. On the basis of the above mentioned considerations he set himself against the Sophists who declared that: "Man is the measure of all things," which is to say that they didn't believe in objective truth, while Socrates held that the truth is objective and that all people apprehend it in the same way. Moreover, he searched in order discover those moral laws that regulate the relations of people. Thus he would reach the point of discoursing on virtue, which had knowledge as a prerequisite. But, again, for someone to reach virtue, one must acknowledge his ignorance and the saying "Know thyself," as the beginning of the path that would lead toward virtue. "Man," he would say, "so long as he cannot know himself, cannot regulate his journey in society, nor can he know which is the path of good and which is the path of evil." With these thoughts Socrates can be justly regarded as the first Athenian philosopher and perhaps the first person who gave a definitive direction to philosophy in respect to morality and to idealism.

Socrates, as a human being, had humor, imagination, spiritual power and a love for truth so strong that at certain times he reached ecstasy. Throughout his whole life he proved his faith and love for his fellow citizens and his fatherland. He lived in great frugality with his small property, didn't seek money for his instruction but literally distributed the richness of his spirit equally among rich and poor. He admonished his brothers to love one another, children to respect and obey their parents, and citizens to be faithful to their fatherland.

The deep moral brilliance of his personality explains the incomparable influence that he exercised on his contemporaries and on the subsequent generations of the world, and especially on his students, of whom Plato (428-347 B.C.) became the primary exponent of the teacher's moral greatness.

The Socratic Method of Study: It was done:

- In conversation with some one of his companions.
- Wherever there was a mass of people (The Agora or market-place, Gymnasiums, Fighting rinks), Socrates was invariably found bound up in dialectical conversation on his beloved subjects. As we previously mentioned, he believed that true knowledge was not only the source but the substance of virtue and he preferred searching for that kind of knowledge which would determine human conduct. For example,:
- What is godliness and what is ungodliness?
- What is beautiful and what is ugly?
- What is noble and what is vulgar?
- What do we mean with the words just and unjust?
- What do we mean by sobriety and insanity?
- What do we mean by courageousness and cowardliness?
- What is a state and what is a politician?
- What is a governor of people and what is a despotic type of person?"

Socrates did not write anything (whatever we know about him derives from the writings of his disciples Xenophon and Plato). He only held conversations. He didn't give lectures or deliver speeches like the Sophists, but, by word of mouth, he compelled others to contradict themselves, to say what they knew and what apprehensions they had for the rules of social behavior. This method they called DIALECTIC. With it Socrates had posited thousands of questions and had no answer for any of them.

Socrates combated the destructive theories of different Sophists and criticized the establishment of the democratic state, saying that Democracy is foolishness and underscored that "it's a ridiculous thing for rulers to be chosen by lot, while no-one ever would dream of choosing by lot a pilot, a builder or whatever other technician, even though the deficiencies of such people are much less detrimental than those which trouble our government."

Thus the wise man created many enemies and was criticized for impiety by the politician Anytus,* the poet Meletus, and the rhetorician Lykonas, and also for corrupting the young. The spokesman for the accusation, which he formulated, was Meletus. The text says "Socrates inflicts injustice by not considering gods those whom the city considers to be gods, and by introducing new demons; he commits injustice also by corrupting the young. The penalty is death."

The issue came before the punitive tribunal, which consisted of 500 lay judges. Socrates left behind a superb monumental speech with Plato's famous *APOLOGY*. But the judges were not persuaded and condemned him to death by the hemlock. Socrates could have avoided the condemnation if he would accept to defend himself or if he implored the mercy of the judges, as this was the custom back then. Not only did Socrates not do something like that, but, when the sage was declared guilty, he proudly and courageously declared that it was impossible to terminate his work of educating the youth, a work which he had performed in accordance with the will of God.

Socrates, when the time came, was surprisingly calm and cool until the last minute, and held the cup of hemlock while, consoling his students who were crying. He drank the poison (399 B.C.) without being disturbed, demonstrating in parallel course a superb disdain of death, because he was sure that he would definitively be cured of the greatest sickness of the soul: The Body.

Truly people (the Athenians), on the one hand, murdered Socrates' body, but they could not murder his soul or the virtues which enlightened and which continue to enlighten peoples' lives. It would not, perhaps, be an exaggeration to say that Socrates became a martyr and saint of Greek history, and that every generation which seeks out an example of a simple life and of courageous thought, drew its ideals from his remembrance.

With the death of Socrates came the end of the Golden Age. Athens became exhausted in body and soul and all the foundations of Athenian life had become irreparably damaged.

* He described Socrates as being the aristocracy's spiritual nourishment.

Some of his thoughts and views:

- Reason is the basis of human nature, and knowledge is the greatest virtue.
- Absolute real knowledge only the gods possess. For this reason man, in this area only knows "that he knows nothing."
- We must look for wisdom and justice, not only because they are useful to us, but additionally because they are pleasing to the gods.
- The gods are everywhere and know all things.
- The world is made for man and every part of human existence is marvelously adjusted towards some good end or purpose. Therefore, the things that exist must be the works of the hands of a wise technician, full of love for all living beings. Because the human being is superior to animals, the Divinity has taken special care for him.
- One thing I know, that I know nothing.
- But now it is time for us to go, I on the one hand to die, and you to live. Which of us journeys towards the better lot no one but God knows.
- Conversation is the symposium of the intellect.
- I always continue learning as I grow old.
- Envy is the ulcer of the soul.
- The human soul more than any other human thing shares in the divine and communes with it.
- In life, as in a long journey, proper rest is indispensable.
- It is better for them to inflict injustice upon you than for you to inflict injustice on them.
- Paideia, (Education, Culture) and virtue, which is the most beautiful thing in the life of humans, is unknown to the many.
- Beauty is a kingdom that reigns for a short while.
- The life of a miser is like a dead person's feasting. Though he has all things, he is not able to taste anything.
- Paideia (culture, education), like a fertile land produces all good things.

HIPPOCRATES
(460-377 B.C.)

The most prominent Greek doctor of antiquity also called the "Great father of Medicine."

He was born in Cos in 460 B.C. and died in Larisa of Thessalia in 377.

He studied at Asklepeio (an altar of Asklepius – an infirmary) of Cos, which was the most significant one of his time and studied further at the medical School of Knidos (an ancient Greek city in Asia Minor) which was then reaching its height. He then visited Thasos, Abdera (an ancient city of Thrace), Kyzikos (an ancient Greek city at Propontida) and other parts of Greece. Moreover, he went about Asia and perhaps Africa and came to know renowned men, like the philosopher Democritus (circa 460-370 B.C.), the rhetorician Gorgias (died in 388 B.C.), and others.

Having gathered valuable observations and conducting serious studies, he returned to his birthplace, where he now gave himself over to the study of the systematic teaching of Medicine and wrote his marvelous works. He died in Larisa of Thessalia and left two sons, Thessalo and Drakonta, both of whom distinguished themselves as doctors.

When Hippocrates appeared, Medicine was a simple art and Magical medicine would, until then, provide therapy, to the sick, while Priestly medicine cared for the sick in the temples of Asclepius, at the Asclypia.

There the priests, who possessed some fundamental knowledge of hygiene and knew of some practical medications, practiced primitive medicine and also performed small surgical operations. Moreover, we should mention that, in certain instances, they also would use suggestion. There was also the School of Gymnasts, who would practice preventative health care, athleticism, diet, bodily aesthetic and performed small surgical operations, as, for example, resetting dislocated joints, straightening fractures, etc. Moreover, there were many experienced doctors, but also philosopher doctors, who, in their studies on nature, also included the human organism.

Hippocrates, having studied all predecessors, with his genius, formulated a new method of study of sicknesses. He studied with care the human organism, especially that of the sick person and studied nature comparatively, imitated it, and experimented on it and used it as a wise guide, a very great doctor, and an unsurpassable teacher. And, thusly, he made medical art into a singular and strictly pure science.

Hippocrates' philosophy of medicine was:

- He believed that every sickness had a physical cause and without physical causes nothing would ever occur.
- He gave great significance to hygiene and particularly to diet.

- He avoided medicines, but at the same time was ready to use them in cases where he considered them completely indispensable.
- When it was necessary he didn't hesitate to use the lancet and to cauterize.
- He elevated the doctor's profession into a kind of sacred function, because he supported the more noble ideals of devotion to duty to the just cause, which resulted, among other things, in doctors today accepting and honoring the Hippocratic oath.

Great figures of his time, like Plato and Aristotle, admired him a great deal, borrowed his opinions and copied his observations.

Hippocrates composed very many theoretical writings concerning different illnesses and organic irregularities, as, for example:

"On Ancient Medicine," "On Dietetic Acids," "Epidemics," "On Juices," "Anatomy," "Physiology," "Pathology," "Diagnostics," "Surgery," "Gynecology," etc.

Many of these things were later sold to the Ptolemians and others were lost, following the fate of all spiritual products of ancient Greek antiquity.

Here we must mention that:

- Until today Medicine, especially as regards diagnostics, follow some of the methods of this great scientist.
- Criticism, both ancient and modern, doubts the genuine and authoritative nature of many of his works.
- Manuscripts of the works of Hippocrates are found in the libraries of Athens, London, Paris, Rome, Vienna, and Berlin etc.

Some of his thoughts and views:

- The doctor must not care at all about his salary, but should care much more about his good renown.
- The idle and lazy are led towards vice.
- In determining his salary the doctor must take into consideration the financial status of the sick person and not ask for excessive amounts in an inhumane manner.
- Every thing in excess is an adversary to nature.
- Where philanthropy exists among doctors also, there too exists the eros or love for science.
- No benefit, either financial or anything else, is as precious as health.

- Study History, my child, because thusly, not only will you glorify yourself and your life and will become valuable to human society, but you will also thus make your mind sharper and clearer.
- Art is lengthy, but life is brief.
- Watered wine stops worry, yawning, shivering. Unwatered wine stops hunger. Generally speaking, wine gives great strength.
- Everything, small or great, executes the function for which it was preordained.

THE HIPPOCRATIC OATH

"I swear to Apollo the doctor and to Asclepius and to Hygeian and Panakean and I invoke the testimony of all the gods and goddesses that I will execute, according to my judgment and according to all my strength, this oath and agreement.

I will look upon him who shall have taught me this Art even as one of my parents. I will share my substance with him, and I will supply his necessities, if he be in need. I will regard his offspring even as my own brethren, and I will teach them this Art, if they would learn it, without fee or covenant. I will impart this Art by precept, by lecture and by every mode of teaching, not only to my own sons but to the sons of him who has taught me, and to disciples bound by covenant and oath, according to the Law of Medicine, and to no-one else.

The regimen I adopt shall be for the benefit of my patients according to my ability and judgment, and not for their hurt or for any wrong.

I will give no deadly drug to any, though it be asked of me, nor will I counsel such, and especially I will not aid a woman to procure abortion.

I will retain my life and Art pure and immaculate.

I will not castrate anyone, even though I am asked to do this, leaving this job to the specialists of this art.

Whatever house I enter, there will I go for the benefit of the sick, refraining from all wrongdoing or corruption, and especially from any act of seduction, of male or female, of bond or free.

Whatever things I see or hear concerning the life of men, in my attendance on the sick or even apart therefrom, which ought not to be revealed to anyone, having as an axiom that such things must remain secret.

In observing, therefore, this oath and not violating it let me have it as a helper throughout my life and in my art, so that I may be highly regarded by all people. But if I violate and break my oath, let me suffer the contrary of the above."

ADMONITIONS TO DOCTORS

"The doctor must have a good external appearance, maintaining his person clean and his clothes well cared for. He must always remain calm and his conduct should inspire trust in the ill person...He must care for himself very much and ... say only what is absolutely necessary...

When you enter into the sick person's room, be attentive to the manner in which you sit, your reservedness, your attire, your decisive speech, the brevity of your words, your calmness...your self-control, your quelling of agitation, your eager willingness to perform whatever needs to be done…I urge you not to be harsh, but to examine with care the economic means of the sick person. Occasionally offer your services for free. And if there is an opportunity to serve a foreigner who is experiencing financial difficulties, provide him with full assistance. For, where there is love towards persons, there too is love for luck."

…If, in addition to all this, the doctor studies and practices Philosophy, he becomes the ideal for his profession. For, "a doctor who loves wisdom is equal to God."

From the above it is most evidently proved that Hippocrates raised the doctor's profession to a ministry, because he supported the noblest ideals of devotion to duty, to the just cause and to love towards man. This resulted, besides other things, in today's doctors accepting and honoring the Hippocratic Oath.

CONCLUSIONS

Hippocrates particularly loved the prognosis (diagnosis) of the illness and its therapy (at its moment of birth) and believed that:

- The good doctor would learn by experience to foresee the consequences of various states of the body and was able to foretell, from the first stages of an illness, the path, which it was about to follow.
- Most illnesses reach a critical point, at which either the illness or the ill person is subdued.
- In every therapy, nature, that is, the powers and the idiosyncracy of the body is the primary healer. The only thing the doctor can do is to subtract or minimize the obstacles to this natural defense and recovery process. Consequently, Hippocratean healing utilizes very few medications, but supports itself primarily on clean air, vomitives, suppositories, enimas, cupping glasses, blood-letting, massages and water-therapy.

"Live a healthy life," Hippocrates advises, and it won't be possible to get sick, except only from an epidemic or an accident. If you get sick, the correct diet will provide you with the greatest possibility for recovery.

Hippocrates recommens "Fasting, if the tolerance level of the sick person allows." For, "the more we feed the ailing bodies, the more we harm them."

DEMOCRITUS
(460-370 B.C.)

Democritus was a famous philosopher of antiquity. The first who conceived of the atomic theory, or else he was taught it by his teacher Leucippus (a Greek materialist philosopher 5th century B.C.), all physical phenomena. This foundation established basis for progress in all the natural sciences. It has led to the interpretation of the laws of sound, light, heat, as well as many of the chemical and physical changes, resulting in the eventual breaking of the atom.)

We may say that the first period of Greek philosophy ended with DEMOCRITUS, who was born at Abdera (an ancient city of Thrace) in 460 B.C. and died, in the same city, in deep old age, in 370.

After a series of lengthy travels that lasted for years (in Greece, in Egypt, in Syria, perhaps also in Persia) and having been cultivated and educated in Asia, he returned to his fatherland, where he lived the life of a hermit, writing, researching and teaching in the school that he established in 420, where he also began to formulate his own philosophical system. Here we must note that he remained for a considerable time in Athens, where indeed he heard Socrates conversing, without however, becoming personally acquainted with him, because he was not at all vainglorious and preferred, like the great cynic philosopher Diogenes, to "Live in obscurity." The same says: "For I came," he said, "to Athens and no-one knew me."

Being very well read and having a broad, universal intellect, he developed, for his time, original views and ideas on the cosmological problem. His new theories and posthumous writing made a great impression on his contemporaries. That's why they called him "pentathlos."

Democritus was a restless person and his love for scientific research was such that he said: "I would have given the entire Persian empire for only a single aitiology – that is, the scientific explanation of a phenomenon. And he continued: "In reality we don't know anything, because truth is buried deep in the Abyss."

He produced very many writings that included all the branches of human knowledge: Mathematics, Physics, Medicine, Agriculture, Ethic, Poetry, Grammar, Music, Painting, Aesthetica, Phonetics, etc. His writings, however, were lost and only a few fragments were saved. From these and from many other sources we know that Democritus held to the view that "Being" (the Universe), on the one hand, is eternal, unchangeable an incorruptible, but, on the other hand, that it is not "simple," like the Eleatic philosophers believed, but a "multiplicity," and considered as basic elements the FULL and the VOID (the empty). According to his teaching the full is separated into innumerable little bodies, which being separated from the void, the one with the other cannot be cut into smaller pieces, because they fill their space and don't have a void within them. These little bodies he would call ATOMS, and he considered them so small that they do not become perceptible by our senses, but only intelligibly and that they have different shapes and sizes but have no starting point or first principle of their existence, but are eternal. Thus, their movement is also eternal. The infinite in number and shape atoms whirl about in the infinite empty space, like dust in the air, and as they are compressed they form infinite worlds (the "Mega Diacosmos"), and the Earth belongs to one of these worlds. And Democritus concludes: There is nothing else true, nothing certain, except for the first elements, that is, the atoms and the void. Only these things exist and operate. Consequently the Universe is nothing other than a continually changing coupling of atoms, which change in three directions: in form, in synthesis, and position (thesis). On this subject he formulated his thought as follows: "The Being is not more real than Non-Being, because the void is not less real than materiality."

In his treatise *Concerning Cheerfulness,* but also in other ones he formulated opinions in the form of maxims concerning the good governance of the state and social morality, etc.

From his work *"Ethics"* there have survived about 230 fragments, most of them maxims, in which Democritus examines practically all moral problems, to which his contemporary Socrates had exclusively turned his attention.

From all of his above opinions, the conclusion emerges that Democritus was not only one of the great thinkers of Greek antiquity, but a man who took an interest in social problematics and formulated some views for their solution.

Here we will have to mention that the life of the wise Abderite is cloaked with the mist of legend and of the mysterious, and many wondrous things are mentioned especially pertaining to the last years of his life by various authors. At all events, one of the characteristic marks of Democritus was that he laughed a lot and at every moment, when seeing how vain and funny were all the serious and important things of humanity before the greatness of the Cosmos. For this reason he was called "Gelesinos" ("Laugher") and the Abedirites worshipped him as a god, and after his death they set up a bronze statue of him.

In other words, the life of the philosopher was a smile. After all, why should it not be, since the world is a stage, life a passing – you came, saw, and left, as he himself would very characteristically say.

Some of his thoughts and views:

- There is not only one spirit, only one God in Nature, but an infinite number of soulish individuals, an infinite number of gods, who with dreams, oracles and other marvelous signs appear to human beings.
- The human being is a small cosmos, a microcosm.
- In the most important matters animals have been our teachers. The spider taught us knitting, the swallow taught us construction, the nightingale and the swan taught us singing.
- Nothing happens according to luck. All things have their cause and happen necessarily.
- Happiness is not found in sheperding, nor in gold; is the soul the seat of happiness.
- It is proper for people to care more for the soul than for the body; because the perfection of the soul restores the body's weaknesses. But the strength of the body, without the strength of prudence, in no way improves the soul.
- To conquer yourself is the first and best victory.
- Good fruits are enjoyed by hard work and labors, while bad fruits are won without labor.
- How much more wise are the animals than us human beings. The animal knows what it has needed of, but the human doesn't know what it has need of.
- Education (culture) for the prosperous is an adornment, but for the unfortunate a refuge.
- Wherever virtue is not appreciated, there vice speaks freely.
- It is a law of nature that the better ones govern.
- The hatred of relatives is more painful than the hatred of foreigners.
- Every place is approachable to the wise person; because the fatherland of the good soul is the whole world.
- Poor is not the person who has few things, but he who desires many things.
- Whoever is a slave to money cannot be just.
- If people did not inflict injustice upon one another, the laws would not obstruct anyone from living however he or she would like to live.
- The purpose of life is cheerfulness, but not that cheerfulness which is identified with pleasure, but the cheerfulness according to which the soul travels with tranquility and calmness, not being disturbed by fear or superstition or by some other passion.
- The first people lived in groups, simply, plainly and with solidarity before the danger of beasts. They all would struggle against the beasts. They didn't know about fire, they didn't have kings and rulers, nor

despots, nor war, nor tyrannies, nor plunderings, but rather they knew a life that was free and plain.

- It is a painful thing to be governed by your inferior.
- The prudent person suffers poverty with dignity.
- The old man was once a young man, but the young man doesn't know if he will become old.
- The grape has three nettles: the first is pleasure; the second is drunkenness, and the third isinsult.

LYSIAS
(459-377 B.C.)

Lysias was a great orator of antiquity. He was born in Athens in 459 B.C., from a Syracusian father. He lived, with small interruptions, in Athens where he also died in 377.

He studied and learned the rhetorical art at Thourios (an ancient Greek colony in Lower Italy), from Teisia, a well-known Syracusian orator. But after the tragic outcome of the military campaign in Sicily, he was compelled to return to Athens in 412.

Though he was a foreign settler, both he and his relatives were admirers and brilliant strugglers for democracy. Thus, when in 404 the democracy was abolished by the thirty tyrants, his family and his relatives were literally dissolved. He just barely survived the hands of the tyrants, escaping to Megara. His property was bound and his brother Polemarchos found a tragic death. From Megara he struggled intensely for the restoration of democracy and most effectively assisted Thrasyboulos (an Athenian general 5th-4th century B.C.) to expel the tyrants.

After the restoration of democracy he returned to Athens where, despite the support of his friends and of Thrasyboulos himself, (who even prompted a vote on the issue), did not succeed in acquiring the right of an Athenian citizen, because the voting was done before the ratification of parliament. For technical, formal reasons we would say today. Thus, from then on, Lysias lived as an “isoteles”.

Through these adverse adventures he became poor, and in order to cover his living expenses he taught rhetoric and wrote speeches on others' account, a “speech-writer” by order. Now because then there were not many legal orators, he became a much sought after advocate; and for this reason he wrote very many speeches. It is said that he wrote about 425, but according to the critics, only 233 of them are considered genuine, of which only 34 have survived and fragments of others. Of these, most are legal (they are delivered by orators at the courts), but Lysias also wrote a few advisory speeches (admonitions for the assembly and Parliament), as well as certain embellished ones (for festivals and celebrations).

The speeches of Lysias that have survived and which mainly belong to the first two decades of the 4th century, show some freshness, power and independence, devoid of rhetorical bonds and follow his own deft art and style. Lysias' writing is a model of simple narration, dramatic skillful artistry in that he adjusts the speech to the character of the speaker, for whom he writes professionally.

Primary characteristics of his speeches are:

- The first and primary virtue, which the more ancient ones praised, is marvelous acting. For, literally, he adjusted his style for each person who would say his speeches, young or old, poor or rich, obscure or glorious, so that his speeches would image the psychological world and character of the speaker, imitating in this way the art of the dramatic poets.
- He used simple and small sentences, with great clarity and without rhetorical forms, as was appropriate for simple people. Let it be noted that brevity was valuable for the attic courts, because time was measured by the Klepsydra (a clay vase, which they used as a time-keeper, from which water dripped in drops).
- He also utilized proverbs with great dexterity, with which he tried to draw the attention and sympathy both of the judges and the audience, on behalf of the speaker.
- They were affected and artistically composed in persuading the judges. That is why it is said that few of them failed in their purpose.
- They were known for their clarity, richness, and strength of proofs, as well as for the brilliance of their ethos.

His most important speeches are the one against Eratosthenes and the one against Agoratus. Of these, the former is worth not only to be read, but also to be studied by all people.

Finally we will have to mention that, because Lysias was occupied with politics, he analyzed the partisan battle going on about the form of the state:

> *"No one by his own nature is a democrat or an oligarch, for each person wants the regime that will serve his own interests."*

How beautiful, but also how prophetic are these positions of Lysias by which, here now for about 2500 years, he sketched, in such a lively fashion, today's Greek voter? Truly, for the human being, though about 25 centuries have passed, continues to think in the same way about certain vital issues, which literally encapsulate his or her entire life. Why has nothing changed from then until now? A great question which awaits a response...

Some of his thoughts and views:

- I think that bodily disasters can be satisfactorily cured by means of psychical virtues (or virtues of the soul).

- It is possible for the powerful, without anything adverse happening to them, to act impudently towards whomever they wish, but it is not possible for the weak, even when they are insulted, to defend against those who made a start of injustice.
- We must utilize as an example all the things that occurred previously in order to decide about what is going to happen in the future.

ARISTOPHANES
(452-385 B.C.)

The most famous and most popular ancient Greek comic, who was born in Athens in 452 B.C., where he lived and rose to distinction.

The poet, in respect to education and mind-set, was a most genuine citizen of Athens. But because, on the other hand, he belonged to the aristocrats, his comedies were full of teasing remarks against the democrats.

As ideal state he considered that of Arsitedes and of Cimon (an Athenian politician and general 510-449 B.C.) and he ridiculed all the demagogues of his day, particularly Cleona (an Athenian demagogue of the 5th century B.C.) calling him a "political monster."

Like Aeschylus, he considered as social prototype the Marathon-warrior. He struggled to bring back again to his fellow citizens the simplicity and piety of those people. It is for this reason, also, that he advises the improvement of public and family nurturing or upbringing, which they had neglected, those same Marathon-warriors, who had evolved into all-cunning sophists, had neglected.

In his comedies he presents this great antithesis between prudent and beautiful *Paideia,* education, and culture and the new, depraved, and undisciplined education of the sophists. Because he hated the sophists, he also ridicules Socrates, whom he confuses with them, as well as Euripides, whose tragedies he regards as sophistical. At all events his disposition to defame two great men of his time was completely inexcusable.

When he was convinced that the deme, the whole deme, had become corrupted, he had the courage to go against it and to ridicule it. Yet the Athenians loved their comic poet so much, that in 405 they crowned him with a soft sacred olive branch, which was considered of equal value to the gold crown.

Aristophanes represents ancient attic comedy, as it was called, whose subjects were not limited to general characters, but more often referred by name to persons and indeed political men whom he ridiculed.

The deamonic poet entered the comic artsat a very young age and dominated on the comic stage of Athens for 40 years, which he truly transformed into a source of cultivation and elevation of the people's spiritual level.

He wrote 40 comedies of which only 11 have survived:

1. The Archarnians (425), where the poet's fervent longing for peace is depicted.
2. Hippes (424), the most biting and powerful drama of Aristophanes' muse, where, with the name Paphlagon, Cleon is literally whipped.
3. The Clouds (423), in which Socrates is satirized.

4. The Wasps (422), where he cauterizes Athenians for being lovers of trials.
5. Peace (421), where he supportsthe pursuit of peace, after the death of Cleon and Brasidas.
6. The Birds (414), where he satirizes the slanderers and demagogues of Athens, on account of whom, the good citizens resort to birds, so that they can live more peacefully between heaven and earth, by building their own city in the clouds.
7. Lysistrata (411), where he seeks, together with the women of Boetia and of the Peloponnese, to abolish nation-destroying war once and for all, since men have proved themselves incapable of doing it.
8. Thesmophoriazusae; Women Celebrating the Feast of Demeter (411), where Euripides is satirized as being a misogynist and slanderer of the female gender.
9. The Frogs (405), a comedy in which the poet judges with such delicacy and grace the two tragedians, Aeschylus and Euripides, so that his opinion, still even today, constitutes the standard for Dramatic Art.
10. Ladies in Parliament (389), the satirizing of ideas pertaining to common possessions for all, which poverty inspired in volatile and arrogant minds. For this reason the poet presents women voting in an assembly on behalf of common property for all.
11. Plutus (388), where he very expressively describes the bad division of wealth, which, being blind, goes to the bad people.

All the works of Aristophanes are distinguished for the abundance of their very funny ideas, their innovative nature, and their fertile imagination. The "sweet laugh" pervades them all, which creates a unique euphoria in the soul, with witty teasing, indecent language, allusions, personal mockings and the ingenious word games, with which he defames the paradoxical and ridiculous things of social and political life – the greediness of the rich, the depravity of the slanderers, the all-cunningness of the sophists, the vileness of the demogogues, the wickedness of the slaves, the charlatanism and greediness of the diviners and priests. He left no one unperturbed.

Finally, the comedies of Aristophanes, also like the tragedies of Aeschylus, Sophocles and Euripides, with their immortal contents, still even today, bear their eternal youth in all theatrical stages of the world.

Some of his thoughts and views:

- The only power that disdains gifts is death.
- Each person's fatherland is where he or she lives better.

- People with prudence many times learn many things from enemies. Prudence is the best guardian.
- It is most irrational for one to fear death, because death is unavoidable for all of us.
- Wealth is extremely cowardly.
- O, old age, how unbearable is your weight to people and, alas!, how bitter you are, for you teach us prudence when we are already weak and powerless to do anything.
- The cunning old man is always contriving new opinions.
- You never find heroes in the dark.

ANTISTHENES
(445-366 B.C.)

Antisthenes was a philospher of ancient Greece, the founder of Cynic Philosophy, who was born in Athens, unknown when. Most probably he was born in 445 B.C. and died 366. He was a contemporary of Plato but older than him. What distinguished him from others was his continence, his calm independence, and his strength of character – virtues which accompanied his frugal, practically ascetic life.

He was a student of Gorgias (a sophist and rhetorician, who died in 388 B.C.) and founded a rhetorical school, even before he had met Socrates, whose pupil he later became, as well as friend and faithful admirer.

After the death of his great teacher, he founded a Philosophical School. He taught at the Kynosarges Gymnasium (high school), which was at a poor and distant Athenian neighborhood. In this gymnasium – which of course was like our schools today – no one whose father or mother was an Athenian citizen was allowed to attend, but only immigrants and children originating from humble descent. ANTISTHENES taught that he faithfully executed that which he taught. We may in describing him say that he was a "Philosopher" of the unfortunate small urbanites and artists not only of Attica, but of the whole Mediterranean corner.

From the name Gymnasium (Cynosarges), but also from the way in which Antishenes' students and followers lived, they were called Cynics (shameless, impudent ones) and their teaching Cynicism (Cynic philosophy).

The most renowned student of Antisthenes, who, for his peculiarities and the disdain he showed for civilization was DIOGENES from Sinopi (413-323 B.C.), who, according to tradition, lived in an earthen cask, with dogs as guards, thus proving that even his house was something superfluous.

In his dialectical and scientific discussions, the philosopher tried to topple Socrates' definition of general ideas. That is to say, he combated Plato's theory concerning ideas and accepted as real only a part of it.

Thus he taught:

> *"Only what we see, touch or feel really exists (aesthesiocratic teaching). The general concepts are nonexistent, and every concept means only one thing, namely, that on which its very name itself is placed."*

From this the philosopher concludes that no *different* idea can be attributed to any subject and that the only correct judgments are tautologies (A is A).

For example, it is not correct to say:

- Gold is blond, but gold is gold.
- The human being is mortal, but the mortal is mortal.

OTHER BASIC IDEAS OF CYNIC PHILOSOPHY

- They didn't accept any social distinctions and its followers (the Cynics) lived an ascetic life with great deprivations DISDAINING EVERY KIND OF WORK.
- Disdaining of wealth.
- He propagandized the motto "Where there is earth there is the fatherland." That is, he anticipated Cosmopolitanism (the life of the cosmopolitan, who often traveled and sojourned in many foreign lands). For this reason also the primary characteristic of the School of the Cynics was that its teachers went about, from city to city and propagandized their ideas with fantisism.
- Virtue is prudence, which is capable of being taught.
- The greatest virtue is SELF-SUFFICIENCY, that is, for each person to limit oneself to what one has. And along with self-sufficiency, FORTITUDE: "for one to patiently endure all things. Whatever obstructs the sense of self-sufficiency is bad; whatever strengthens it is good. That's why people must return to the primitive state, the primitive life, to nomadic life, far from the cursed cities, where debauchery and immorality reign.

The cynics eagerly embraced these teachings and tried to make themselves completely independent of daily needs, exercising themselves in enduring every want and every pain, and at the same time considering enjoyments, especially pleasure, very evil things.

Antisthenes, if we are to believe tradition, wrote many books, and according to Diogenes Laertius (a Greek author of the 3rd century A.D.), these comprised up to ten volumes. Unfortunately, as occurred with almost all the ancient philosophers, his work was lost. Only a few fragments and phrases survived.

Some of his thoughts and views:

- The greatest virtue is self-sufficiency.
- Virtue is a weapon that cannot be taken away.
- Virtue is enough for you to be happy.
- The wise person must not govern according to laws, but with the laws of virtue.

- It is preferable for you to fall prey to a crow ("koraka"), than to flatterers ("kolakes"). Crows devour the dead person's body, and flatterers devour the living person's soul.
- I'm looking to find a human being.
- The cohabitation of beloved brethren is more powerful than any wall.
- Those who want to be immortal must live with godliness and justice.
- The most necessary lesson of all is to unlearn all the bad lessons.

XENOPHON
(445-354 B.C.)

Xenophon was a famous historian, philosopher, author and an excellent general.

He was born in 445 B.C. (according to others in 430), to a well to do family with conservative tendencies. From his social environment he assimilated the feelings that distinguished his class and which closed within them the scholastic respect for the external elements of religion, moral thought, some delicateness of feeling and of reason, the interest for military training and outdoor athletics, the courage and devotion to his class. In other words, he was a genuine representative of Greek chivalry.

He traveled a great deal and acquired much knowledge of the world and with the broadness of his intellect, his liberal education and his ethical and religious principles he represents the best characteristics of the educated class of his generation.

Here we must note that as a youth, he was a student of Socrates, toward whom he was always devoted and had limitless gratitude and who, besides others, also contributed to the formation of his character.

He demonstrated a great deal of prudence, courage, and fortitude and simultaneously unfolded all his military virtues, when, after the defeat of Cyrus at Kounaxa by Artaxerxis, he led, with very many difficulties and adversities, from the heart of Asia, through enemy races and distant deserts, the thousands of Greek soldiers, to Byzantio, and later to Pergamus (an ancient Greek city in Asia Minor), where he gave them up to the Spartan general Thimbronas, who had undertaken a campaign against the Persian Satraps, Tissaphernes and Pharnavazou. Then, in the spring of 396 he accompanied the Spartan King Agesilaus, who was conducting a campaign in Asia, and participated, in his following at the battle of Koroneia (394).

These actions of his resulted in the Athenians criticizing him as "laconizing," that is to say, that he sympathized and supported the Laconians-Spartans, and they exiled him. He settled in Corinth, where he remained, and after his exile was revoked he died in deep old age in the year 354 B.C.

His works, which are products of his deamonic spirit and full of sublime ideas, are historical, historico-political, philosophical and practical and are important sources for the history of ancient Greece.

The most significant of these are:

- The "Anabasis of Cyrus," which narrates the military campaign of Cyrus and especially the coming down of the Thousands, in which he gives us the synthesis and the psychology of the mercenary army, which had been made up from different parts of Greece and which passed through various phases of success, misadventures and dangers.

- "The Paideia of Cyrus," that is, the upbringing of Cyrus, which is an ethico-political and historic story, in which the author presents a certain prototypical education of the child who, on the basis of Socratic principles, can be developed into the ideal man and ruler.
- The political ones: "The Lacedaimonian State" and "Athenian State."
- "The Memorabilia of Socrates," a philosophical work, which consists of four books, in which Xenophon supports the teacher against the accusations of impiety and corruption of the youth,
- The "Memoirs," where he presents Socrates' image in daily life.
- The "Symposium of Philosophers," in which he presents Socrates in a cheerful company dining together and developing his philosophical thoughts.

Some of his thoughts and views:

- Of all present things, none are given by the gods to people without labor and effort.
- When the citizens obey the laws, then cities become all-powerful.
- Whoever wants to live, let him or her try to overcome.
- Poverty, bad upbringing and lack of education lead people to evil.
- The gods give nothing good and beautiful to human beings unless they themselves make strong efforts and take great cares.
- I consider happy the person who obtains money without inflicting injustices and uses it for good and beneficial works.
- He who governs and holds the universe together, in which all things are good and beautiful, who maintains it eternally incorruptible, undisturbed and unaging, and whose will more quickly obeys his thought, he is the one who becomes known through his great works, though he remains invisible.
- The more ancient human establishments, the wisest nations are those in which religion dominates. The more enlightened centuries are those in which the people devoted their greatest cares to the gods.
- Discipline is a great good; when one is disciplined one can create good works.
- Agriculture is the mother and nurturer of every art.
- The sweetest sound of all is praise.
- The only person among human beings that is rich is the person who is self-sufficient.
- Not a single human being is to be found who will live his whole life without worries.

ISOCRATES

(436-338 B.C.)

The fourth in line in the series of renowned attic orators is Isocrates, who was born in 436 B.C. at Athens, where he lived and died, in deep old age at 338.

The duration of his life coincided with the entire evolution of prose literature and with the peak of the city-state, but also with the beginning of its decline.

He was the son of the wealthy Theodoros the flute-maker and thus had the chance to luck upon a good and meticulous upbringing and *Paideia*, education and cultivation. He was distinguished for his genius and his love of learning and he studied with the then famous sophists and orators (Gorgias, Teisias), and even was a student of Socrates, but, he wasn't yet prepared for the study and examination of metaphysical issues and neither had he inclinations for Dialectic, which, indeed, he disdained.

Initially (402-393) he began as a Speech-writer, and from his pen 6 speeches have survived. A bit later (390) he established a Rhetorical School, whose program is incoperated into his inaugural speech against the sophists and with which he promised to raise his students to distinction, to become not only wise and good orators, but also men capable of apprehending ideas in their mind and to act rightly. For this purpose, in a series of lessons, which lasted three or four years, he educated his students in Rhetoric and he equipped them with substantial knowledge useful for excelling in various public careers.

His students, who were exceptionally endowed young men from distinguished families, would come from all parts of Greece, as well as from distant regions, like the Black Sea, Cyprus, and Sicily. After having completed this education, many of them became Philosophers, Speech-writers, Orators (Isaeus, Lycurgus, Aeschynes and Hepereides), Politicians (Timothy and Leodamas), Historians (Theopompos of Chios and Ephoros of Kymaius), Generals and even Kings. Besides these, the young man who would graduate from his school had to have a broad intellect, which looked to the interest not only of his respective city of birth, but of the entire Greek Nation.

The School of Isocrates was most significant. This resulted in its gaining very wide and great fame, which drew about it powerful persons. It was related even to the King of Cyprus Evagoras, Archidamus of Sparta, and Philip of Macedonia. The value of Isocrates' teaching is attested to also by the fact that his students paid the huge amount for tuition at that time of a thousand drachmas.

Isocrates loved democracy, praised Pericles, but also greatly admired Solon. As a person he was peaceful, polite, noble and dispassionately judged matters not only of his own fatherland but also of all Greece, without bad-mouthing other cities. And he advised, in every way, friendship and harmony, achieving the same mind-set.

He died while performing a hunger strike in deep old age in 338, that is, at the age of 98.

The speeches of Isocrates, which are sublime, grandiose and of Panhellenic significance and interest, excel in brilliance and nobility of subject-matter, and only in his later works is some elderly verbosity discerned. The Athenians experienced particular pleasure on account of the beauty and grace of Isocrates' speeches and both the friends and enemies of the orator tried to imitate his speeches.

Truly, even today, when one reads his speeches, one is greatly impressed and the reader is easily drawn in and gripped by the ideas, the beautiful rhythm, and the most skillfull, artistic synthesis of his discourse.

The authentic speeches of Isocrates, according to Dionysus of Alicarnassos,* are 25, which are: 6 legal, 3 exhortations, 14 oratorical and 2 against the sophists. Of these 21 have come down to us, as well as 9 letters to prominent personages. Besides these, he wrote the significant work "Rhetorical Art," which the ancients very greatly valued, but unfortunately, of this only a few fragments have survived.

His most important discourses are:

- The "Panegeric" (380), which in its conception of ideas and in phraseology is excellent and is very strongly set against the Spartans, who, on account of their great regionalism, created obstacles against the undertaking of panhellenic war against the barbarians. It is said that toward this purpose he worked ten whole years. The speech contained feelings that could be interpreted as cosmo-political, though the meaning of one of his most famous statements appears to be, simply, that culture has become more of a characteristic feature of Greece than tribal affliation. He would say: "So much has our city left the rest of humanity behind it in thought and expression, that its citizens have become teachers of others and have made the name "Greek" a distinguishing mark no longer on account of descent, but on account of intellectual orientation, and has become the reason for them to be called Greeks, that is, those who share in our civilization than in our common descent."
- "On Peace" (353), where he supports a peace-seeking policy and propagandized peace and advised Athenians, not only to achieve peace

* A technographer and Historiographer (1st century B.C.)

and to radically change their foreign policy, but to definitively abandon the politics of naval rule.

- "Areopagitikos" (354), where he argues that the Athenian state must be reformed and for the regime that had prevailed at the time of Solonos and Cleisthenis to return.
- "Antidoseos" (346), where he treats a dual idea: to work toward harmony among the Greeks, and Greek unity as well as in their struggles against the barbarians.
- "The Panathenaikos" (399), which constitutes Isocrates' tragic plea for Panhellenic union and the prevalence of ancient practical wisdom.

Some of his thoughts and views:

- The roots of education are bitter, but its fruit is sweet.
- One evil deed done is followed by thousands of evils.
- Authority, which all seeks, is difficult to handle and makes insane those who love it. It is like women lovers who elicit love and lead their lovers to destruction.
- Admonish your younger people in virtue not only with good advise but, above all, with your example.
- You learn who your true friends are in a time of misfortune.
- Prefer poverty that comes with justice to wealth that comes from injustice.
- Beautiful is the triumph of the statuesque quality of the body, but more beautiful is the triumph of the soul and the spirit.
- Hate flatterers precisely as you hate deceivers.
- Imitate the actions of those whose glory you envy.
- Don't ridicule anyone found in misfortune, for fate is common to all and the future is unknown.
- Think carefully, but quickly excecute your decisions.
- Nothing is more modest and more certain than virtue.
- Nature granted glorious death as a gift to the virtuous.
- Justice is so much better than other things, since things benefit those who live, but justice glorifies even those who have died.
- From the use of common things come away not richer, but more glorious.
- Conduct yourself pleasantly towards all, but associate with the excellent ones.
- If you are a lover of learning, you will learn a great deal.
- Be such towards your parents, as you would have wished your children to be towards you.
- Fear slanders, even if they are false.

- Love not to obtain many goods, but to enjoy them with the measure they dictate.
- Reflect that, whatever you do, you won't escape anyone's attention.
- Zeal that is not accompanied with a practical spirit is fire without radiance.

ARISTIPPUS
(435-350 B.C.)

Aristippus was one of the wise men of ancient Greek thought who founded his own philosophical school: the famous Cyrenaic or School of Pleasures ("Hedonikon"). He was born in Cyrene (an ancient Greek city in North Africa) around 435 B.C. and died about 350.

He came to Athens at a mature age in order initially to study with Protagoras and later Socrates, without, however, renouncing his own theories.

The basis of Aristippus' theory was simple. The center of his philosophical theory is pleasure ("hedone"). But pleasure is psychical or soulish activity and bodily enjoyment. In other words, he doesn't deny pleasure as being a spiritual state, but he considers spiritual pleasure to be inferior to bodily pleasure.

Thus he taught: "Whatever we do we do with the hope of enjoyment or the fear of pain – even in the case we become poor for the sake of our friends or give our life for the sake of our generals. And he would conclude: Consequently, according to general acceptance, enjoyment is the final good and every other good, including that of Virtue and of Philosophy, must be judged in proportion to its capability to offer us enjoyment...

And he completes his thought by concluding that the prudent person must show respect towards the common opinion and to the laws, and to "persistently try as much as possible not to be either lord nor slave to any human being."

Aristippus, who was beautiful in form, delicate in his manner of conduct and ingenious in his speech, succeeded not only in separating his influence everywhere, but, as Diagenes Laertius writes (a Greek author of the 3rd century A.D.), he knew how to deal with occasion, so that he easily won the good-will of the powerful. For this reason Diogenes the wise man called him "Royal dog."

CHARACTERISTIC MARKS OF THE SAGE:

- After the death of Socrates, he is the first of his pupils who would get paid for his teaching.
- He didn't hesitate to flatter even the tyrants in order to achieve his aim.
- When the tyrant of Syracuse Dionysius I spit in his face, he smiled with patience and said: "A fisherman must suffer much more humidity than this, when he is about to apprehend even the smallest fish."
- When a friend of his criticized him for kneeling before Dionysius he answered that: "It wasn't his mistake that the tyrant had his ears on his feet."

- He felt disdain towards those people who sought riches for the sake of riches.
- When the wealthy Simos from Phrygia (an ancient land of Asia Minor) once showed him his luxurious home, which was strewn with famous marbles, Aristippus spat on his face; and to Simos' protest, he excused himself saying that: "Among all those famous marbles he didn't find a more appropriate place to spit."
- When he was once reproached for living with a concubine he answered: "He didn't object to living in a house or traveling on a ship that others had used before him."

Without a doubt, his raw hedonism was due, in part, to his pleasure in scandalizing the dignified sinners of the city. This is not due to chance because he worshipped Socrates and particularly loved Philosophy.

Despite all his eccentricities the world loved him because, besides his other gifts, he was a man of good, noble, and delicate manners, of great spiritual cultivation and a good heart.

Aristippus wrote many works. The most significant ones are the following: "Artabaszos," "To the Shipwrecked," "To fugitives," "To the poor," "Another Question," "To Intimates" or "Pros Oikeious."

Some of his thoughts and views:

- Parents must arm their children with wealth, which, after a shipwreck, will enable them to swim dry land. (This is an allegorical meaning given to wealth. He is referring to spiritual equipment – that is, good and correct education).
- Don't ascribe value to anything, so long as you can do without it. (He left this as the greatest inheritance to his daughter before his death.)
- The most imposing sight in life is the vision of a virtuous person who steadily follows his or her own pathway among the corrupt.
- The art of life is in experiencing the enjoyments as they come, and to use them as much as possible, whenever the moment provides.
- Only the present exists, which most probably is as good as the future, if not better.
- Man must rejoice in enjoyments without being a slave to them, and must with prudence be able to distinguish between those that expose him to danger and those that do not.
- The purpose of Philosophy is not for it to turn us away from enjoyments, but rather to lead us to their most pleasant choice and use.
- Don't sacrifice a present good for the sake of a hypothetical future good.

PLATO
(428-347 B. C.)

A renowned creative philosopher of his time who, along with Aristotle (384-322 B.C.), initiated in the fourth century the world-wide domination of the Greek spirit and at the same time established the foundations for a new epoch. He was born in 428 B.C. in Athens, where he also died at the age of 81 (347).

As a young man he initially occupied himself with Poetry, but quickly he definitively applied himself to Philosophy, because on his path then appeared Socrates (470-399 B.C.), who charmed him and drew him away from Poetry. He followed his teaching for nine years and was able to comprehend from all sides the personality and the philosophy of his teacher and to become one of the greatest fashioners of the human soul.

Plato is distinguished for his depth and multi-faceted nature. He shone as a literary stylist and created a new literary form, the Dialogue, in which there is a representation of the living word performed with exemplary grace. In his Dialogues are treated problems concerning the intellectual, moral and political life of people.

His was an uneasy spirit and his thirst for learning was great. For this reason he traveled, during which times he met with many philosophers, especially of the Pythagorean School.

When at forty years old he returned to Athens, he founded a regular school, the so-called ACADEMY, which took its name from the place that was dedicated to the mythical Attic hero, Acadimo. PLATO taught in his academy for about 42 years.

Plato's primary interest was ethics. Thus, like Socrates, he tried to make society moral and to implement his ideas not only by oral speech, but also by written discourse. He tried to spread his political ideas for the better organization of the nation.

In his works, *The Republic, The Laws, The Statesman, The Sophist,* and *The Apology* of Socrates, which are also the most important and constitute masterpieces of attic discourse, he formulates his political ideology and various other theories for dealing with the problems of society. However, in these as well as in others (he wrote 36 works) he also formulates his philosophical views – ideological idealism (philosophical-dogma, according to which the visible world is a product of imagination [sic] and exists only in cognition) – which marked an important stage in the History of ancient Greek Philosophy.

Thus, the basis for his philosophical thought was "THE IDEAS," which he sets beyond the physically sensible things which are corruptible. The Ideas, for Plato, are incorruptible and eternal, outside of place and time and are apprehended only by reason. This is to say he taught that, outside of us and generally outside of the material world there exists the spirit, which is, so to speak, a refulgence of morality and which governs material nature.

The teaching of Plato at the Academy referred:

- to the world of matter
- to the world of the senses and
- to the world of the real BEING, which consists of incorruptible beings, the "IDEAS" about which he taught:

"The greatest of his ideas is God, who created the world and gave it a soul, making it from the same essence as the cosmic soul; though less pure, from within which reason, order, and life pervaded all things."

In Plato's theory the body is only the dark cell or tomb of the soul, which must be purified of the body in order to achieve the good and virtue, which means for the soul to become suitable to its primary task. In developing, moreover, the teaching regarding the immortality of the soul, he led the thought of contingent man towards the eternal and incorruptible.

In conclusion we may say that it is not knowledge that PLATO discovered, but his Faith in spiritual realities, his desire for the beautiful, the fine and the true; his understanding about the tremendous heights that a human being can reach and which place him or her among the strong spiritual and moral powers that exercise their energy upon the human race.

Some of his thoughts and views:

- By means of cultivation, the human being advances towards the highest Good, which is neither knowledge, nor happiness, but becoming like unto God to the greatest possible degree. Happiness, being completely different from bodily pleasure, is the acquisition of good.
- The name of "sage" appears great to me and is appropriate only to God.
- It is difficult for one to discover the maker and father of the universe, and if one does discover him, it is impossible for one to reveal him to others.
- If a human being is brought up correctly, he or she becomes the most noble and calm creature. If, however, he or she doesn't receive sufficient and appropriate cultivation, he or she becomes the most wild animal of nature.
- The beauty of the soul is a value of greater honor and worth than the beauty of the body.

- The child is the most difficult beast to manage; for, to the degree its spiritual powers have not developed sufficiently, it becomes wilder, more aggressive, and more dangerous than the beasts. For this reason it must be bridled.
- Instruct the children by playing with them and not by force.
- The greatest thing of all is health, the second greatest is psychical beauty, or beauty of the soul, and the third is to become rich without using deceit.
- It is difficult and very meritorious for one to live justly when indeed one has the power to inflict injustice upon others.
- The lie is hated by the gods and by human beings.
- It is necessary for people to set down laws and to live according to them. Otherwise, people in no way differ from the wild beasts.
- What person would be capable of liking a city without laws?
- The cities and citizens will prosper only when philosophers become kings or when kings become philosophers.
- The state is nourishment for people: good nourishment for the good people, and bad nourishment for the bad people.
- Justice is a virtue of the state.
- Virtue has many teachers but few practitioners.
- Independence in thought is the noblest form of pride.
- People's upbringing must include bodily as well as spiritual training.
- Paideia is the second sun for people.
- Cultivation calms everyone down.
- Music is a moral law. It gives soul to the universe; it elevates the imagination, expels the bad disposition, and gives joy to life. It is the essence of orderliness and leads to whatever is good, just, and beautiful.
- Eros minimizes misanthropy, increases friendliness, organizes entertainments, is the first at celebrations, at dances, and at rites. He brings goodness, and expels brutishness. He is open-handed in good-will, and a miser in ill-will. He is affectionate, good, the pride of sages, boast of the gods. He is the father of nourishment, of politeness, of luxury, of graces, of passion, and of yearning. He is sleepless for the good, indifferent for the bad. In every pain, fear, longing, he is pilot, sea-fighter, warrior, and an excellent savior. He is the adornment of all the gods and people, whom each person must follow, singing the same song which he sings, charming the mind of gods and people.

DIOGENES
(413-323 B.C.)

Diogenes was a famous cynic philosopher of ancient Greece. He was par excellence the representative of cynic philosophy. He was born in Sinopi (an ancient Greek sity of Euxonos Pontus), in 413 B.C. and died at Corinth, in deep old age in 323 B.C.

As a young man he came to Athens to study with the founder of the cynic school of philosophy Antisthenes (445-366 B.C.), of whom he became the most beloved and faithful student. Truly, DIOGENES was the most renowned student of Antisthenes because of his peculiarities and the disdain that he showed towards civilization: he taught disdainment of riches, and the return of people to nature. He didn't accept social distinctions and lived an ascetic life with great wants, DISDAINING EVERY FORM OF WORK. Thus, with his example, he showed that he faithfully performed the things that he taught. In other words, he was perhaps the unique person who executed the theories of his teacher most faithfully in action.

DIOGENES passed his days in the market-places and at cross-roads and according to tradition lived in an earthen cask, where he lived with the dry bread that they threw him. He had dogs as his guards, thus demonstrating that even the house is something superficial.

Here I think it is worth remembering that when Alexander the Great (356-323 B.C.) entered Athens as an invader (335 b.C.), he asked to see Diogenes, whose fame had reached Macedonia. And when they led him to Diogenes' dwelling at the entrance of the stadium and he saw the sage sitting outside his cask, full of enthusiasm and sympathy he asked him to express some desire. And Diogenes, without throwing him a second glance, and disturbed a bit, gave the famous reply:

"Move over a bit, because you're blocking the sun."

Then, it is said, Alexander said:

"By Jove, if I were not Alexander, I would want to have been Diogenes."

This paradoxical philosopher made a philosophical vocation out of the rogue, vagabond life (he lived without working, as a beggar and man of the street). When they once asked him why he was a cosmopolitan (i.e., a citizen of the world), he answered: "The only correct way of life is the life lived in the world. These things Diogenes Laertius informs us (a 3rd century A.D. Greek author). Epictetus (A Greek stoic philospher 50-120 A.D.), also informs us that Diogenes used to say: "All land is fatherland, and there is no exception" and as well as the motto: "wherever there is land there is fatherland." He was also said to love people and suffered all the worse for misfortunes to the common good.

From the above it is most evident that the life of Diogenes was most frugal, and the Athenians loved him very much for his readiness and genius, with which he answered every question they put to him, as well as for the unyielding, rough and harsh manner with which he ridiculed the bad state of affairs in society. The socio-ethical problems were what occupied his mind, and his teaching essentially was revolutionary and overturning of the existing order.

Diogenes would say that he considered himself called by the Dephic oracle: "To inscribe the coin." Thus he believed that the real meaning of the oracle was that he must try to make a radical change and transformation of human society and of corrupted human nature. People, he observed, have been formed by nature with a noble metal, which, however, circumstances have debased. That is why it must be reminted and re-inscribed (for the metal to be remelted), in order for the human being to again become an image of God and to acquire again the highest form of happiness, which is the primary aim of virtue. As the main representative of cynic philosophy, he taught, like his teacher Antisthenes, that people must again return to nature, that is, to the primitive state, the primitive life, to simple, nomadic life, far from the cursed cities, where debauchery and immorality reigns. Nature, he would say, equipped the human being, as well as other creatures, with all the indispensable things needed to live, but it created unsatisfiable desires and needs which often lead to wickedness and corruption.

Concerning the spiritual work of Diogenes, Diogenes Laertius provides us with the presentation of a very small list of his works, from which, however, nothing has survived. The same chose maxims, anecdotes, and details from the life and works of the great cynic philosopher.

Some of his thoughts and views:

- The natural and frugal life is incomparably more pleasurable than the life of the civilized person, who chases after technical pleasures and lives a more miserable life than that of the animals.
- The other dogs bite the enemies, but I bite friends in order to save them.
- People pray to the gods for health, but most people do things contrary to their health.
- The noblest of people are those who disdain riches, glory, pleasure, and life.
- Virtue cannot dwell either in a rich city, or in a rich home.
- Cultivation is for the young prudence, for the aged a consolation, for the poor wealth, and for the wealthy an adornment.

PECULIARITIES OF THE ECCENTRIC SAGE:

As known, Diogenes resorted to begging from a real need (he was a banker from Sinopi who had gone bankrupt) and with pleasure realized that this constitutes virtue and wisdom. From then:

- He wore the clothing and carried the cane of the beggar and he lived in an earthen cask, in the outer court of the goddess Kybelis (mother of Zeus).
- He envied the simple life of animals and tried to imitate it (truly he lived the simple life with such consequence that he became the most famous man of Greece, after Alexander the Great.)
- He would sleep on the dirt, eat whatever he found wherever he would find it. And what is strangest of all: it is said he fulfilled his physical and amorous needs in public.
- Sometimes he held a lantern and would say: I seek a human being (this was not an eccentricity of the cynic philosopher, but an allegory with deep philosophical meaning, for even today, about 2400 years later, truly a human being is being sought after…)
- He reproached a woman who would bend down with her head on the ground before a certain sacred icon, as follows: "Are you not afraid that you might be found in an immodest position, if there is some god behind you, since this place is full of gods?"
- When he saw the child of a concubine throwing rocks against the multitude he said to him: "Be careful you don't hit your father."
- When a Corinthian youth, with rich gaudy clothes and smelling of cologne put a question to him, Diogenes said: "I won't answer before you tell me whether you are a boy or a girl."
- When Alexander the Great met Diogenes laying down in the Sun, the monumental dialogue became known. I set forth the first two paragraphs:
  I am Alexander, the great king, said the monarch.
  And I am Diogenes, the dog, said the philosopher…
- When a priest explained to Diogenes how many things the virtuous would enjoy after death, he asked him:

  "Then why don't you die?"
  (the cynics didn't believe in the gods)

His Noteworthy and Famous Views:

- The only true philosophy is morality.
- The modest and virtuous life is the only path of steady satisfaction.
- Only internal freedom has importance.
- The gods gave the human being an easy life, but the human being made it complicated with the mania of luxury.
- Civilization was a mistake and Prometheus (a mythical son of the first god of Heaven and Earth, who stole fire from Zeus and gave it to human beings) was worthy of crucifixion, because he brought fire to humans.

ANTIPHANES
(405-333 B.C.)

Antiphanes was one of the most widely mentioned poets of middle comedy. He was born in Asia Minor or Rhodes and acquired the political rights of the Athenian citizen at Demosthenes' recommendation.

It is calculated that he wrote 260 comedies and according to others 365, but he came in first place only 13 times.

Many of his comedies were performed only at the theatre of Athens. For this reason the idea circulated that he was writing many of these comedies for foreign theatres.

Besides, it is known that at that time theaters had been established in the entire Greek peninsula, as well as in the Greek colonies.

Characteristic features of the poet:

- He had a very sharp mind and possessed great readiness in both beautiful writing and in writing drama.
- He wanted to write many things and for this reason he repeated the same things (subjects).
- His comedies had more of a rhetorical pathos than a poetic value.
- Though he was not a born Athenian, he used the attic dialect skillfully and gracefully.

Of his comedies only fragments have survived, in which symposiums are described in detail, but also particularly good opinions are formulated with precision, as, for example:

- Everything serves work.
- The merchant nurtures a great idea about money, while the wind often is the lord of all.
- Let us not sorrow excessively for friends who depart; one day we too will take the same path.
- Old age is a workshop in which all evils are manufactured.
- It is better to be poor than get rich by dishonorable means. For, poverty draws sympathy, but wealth draws condemnation.
- What are we but mercenaries of death, since we live in order to die?
- The hunger of the soul doesn't cease with brilliant dinners.
- Melancholy is the nearest neighbor to insanity.
- Most of the time, people inflict injustice whenever they are able to do so.
- Neither a single clear day, nor a single swallow makes summer.
- You make learning your property by means of labor…

- It is not a good thing for the person who has not been governed to govern.
- All are friends to those who prosper, but not even parents are friends to those who suffer misfortune.
- All things are found to be in ceaseless movement.
- The soul of a city is nothing other than the state, which has as much power as prudence does in respect to the body.
- Change is a form of rest.
- Power is sweet.
- All things subject themselves to diligent study.
- Every form of slavery is contrary to nature.
- It is a fearful evil in the human being to laugh out of season, without reason.

XENOCRATES
(396-314 B.C.)

Xenocrates was an ancient Greek philosopher. He was born in Chalcedon (an ancient Greek city on the Bosporus) in the 4th century B.C. He was a student of Plato and headmaster of the Academy from 339-314 B.C.).

It is said that he was a man with an impressive personality, who combined strict dignity with nobility and who exercised particular charm on his students and conversants.

In the year 332 B.C. he was sent as ambassador of Athens to the Macedonian Antipater.

As basic and first principles of his theory he accepted THE ONE (the superabundant) and the TWO (the whole), which, however, he interpreted also as being divinities, one masculine and the other feminine (ZEUS and HERA).

His philosophy was rather a weak attempt at developing Platonic philosophy into a system of forms, without becoming distanced from the essence of the great philosopher, whose idealism, nevertheless, he was unable to apprehend.

Besides this, he was interested in examining the nature of the gods and of deamons and to interpret their relations to the heavenly bodies, in a way that reminds one of the subsequent thought of the Neoplatonists.

Yet, he was basically concerned with moral issues, of a practical nature. Being influenced by the Pythagorians, he occupied himself with the "indivisible lines."

Modern students consider him to be a typical representative of the ancient Academy and a brilliant teacher, rather than an intellectual in his own right.

He wrote a good amount of works and occupied himself particularly with Geometry, especially its history.

Of his work only very few fragments have survived.

Some of his thoughts and views:

- Avoid the company of very talkative people.
- Don't ruin your friendship because of a small transgression of your friend.
- When you are angry, don't say anything or do anything.
- Don't allow yourself to be tortured by sorrows.
- Don't poke the fire with the knife. That is, don't light up a person who is already angry.
- There is nothing more respectable than the quality of being a father.

HYPERIDES
(390-322 B.C.)

A chief Athenian orator, one of the ten of the "canon," that is, he was among those names included on the tablet which the learned of Pergamus (an ancient Greek city in Asia Minor, a famous spiritual center) had drawn up to designate the most significant Attic orators. He was born in Athens in 390 B.C. and died in Aegina in 322 after being tortured.

He was a student of Isocrates and Plato. In his life, however, he held views contrary to the teachings of his teachers, being independent in respect to politics, but, with courageousness and fervent zeal, he supported the interests of the city.

His political principles then became known, when he accused Philocrates (the spokesman who signed the peace treaty with Philip, who was called "Philocrateus" – 346 B.C.) of betrayal, who was then condemned. From then on fearlessly and without monetary remuneration, together with Demosthenes, battled against those bribed by Philip to favor the Macedonian policies.

Hyperides was a contemporary and fellow combatant of Demosthenes in the struggle against Macedonian domination. He remained till the end, immovable from his positions of the liberal party, which represented the anti-macedonian party (portion) of the Athenian people, and he didn't hesitate to indict even his fellow combatant and friend with similar views, Demosthenes, when he believed that he had been bribed by the enemy and had betrayed the common struggle.

He began his political activity in 360 B.C., at an exceptionally critical time for Hellenism, because Philip skillfully manipulated the weakness and jealous rivalries of the Greek cities, in order to enforce his will and to extend his domination in Southern Greece.

As is well known, the soul of the anti-macedonian struggle was Demosthenes. Hyperides, though five years older, would recognize Demosthenes' primacy and a slightly prison to the battle of Chaeroneia (338 B.C.), proposed that Demosthenes be crowned with a golden crown for his many services to the city.

After the death of Philip the Athenians and the Thebans united against Alexander the Great. To this alliance Hyperides also contributed, and later prompted the Athenians to declare war against Alexander the Great.

In 324, Hyperides came into dispute with Demosthenes, occasioned by their disagreement regarding the proposals of Arpalus (a secretary treasurer of Alexander the Great), who, in order to avoid expulsion for abuses (he stole treasures of the King) came to Athens and offered assistance in the form of money and mercenaries, when Athens was about to revolt against Alexander.

Hyperides favored accepting this proposition and Demosthenes was against it. Surely Arpalus was jailed at the Acropolis, and his money – 5,000 talents – was confiscated, so it could be returned to Alexander. When Arpalus escaped, a significant amount of this money was missing. Hyperides accused Demosthenes. In the speech he delivered against him, he mentioned that Demosthenes destroyed the friendship that had joined them, because he took money to turn against his fatherland. Thus, he would continue saying, the same person, Demosthenes, became worthy of mockery and brought shame upon his previous companions in the struggle. Demosthenes was condemned by the court of Eleas (a lay court consisting of 6,000 citizens) to pay a fine of 50 talents, and because he didn't have it, he fled. After this, Hyperides became the leader of the anti-macedonian party.

After the death of Alexander the Great (323 B.C.), Hyperides moved swiftly in order to organize a struggle against his successors in Macedonia, Antipater and Craterus. Then he was reconciled with Demosthenes, who returned to Athens, where he became accepted with great honors. But his attempt against Antipater failed. For this reason, after the fall, which the Athenians suffered in the Lamian war, they were compelled to accept the establishment of the Macedonian guard in Mounychia (Castella-Tourkolimano). Later Antipater also asked for the surrender of the leaders of the panmacedonian party, from which all had already left, and Hyperides, together with his co-workers, took refuge in Aegina. He hid within a sacred temple of the city, but Archias (Thebaios the oligarch), after having removed him from the temple gave him up to Antipater, by whom he was killed after torturing. Indeed it is said he had ordered that his tongue be cut out.

Hyperides the orator had enjoyed great admiration and people praised his grace, as they did the power of Demosthenes, who had been considered the Zeus of Rhetoric. He wrote many speeches, but the ancients attributed 77 to him, from which 52, perhaps, were genuine, but only fragments of them have survived.

The most well known of his speeches are: "Against Demosthenes," "On behalf of Lycophronos", "Against Philip," "Against the Athenian race" and "Funeral Oration," which he delivered in order to honor Leosthenis and the other Athenians who fell during the Lamian war.

Some of his thoughts and views:

- Philip considers himself to be a Panhellenic leader.
- He admonished the Athenians and other cities of southern Greece to move against Philip and the Macedonian rulership.
- Philip seeks the political union of Hellenism.

AESCHYNES
(389-314 B.C.)

Aeschenes was one of the ten attic orators (Lysias, Antiphontas, Andokides, Isocrates, Iseos, Lycurgus, Demosthenes, Aeschynes, Hyperides and Denarchos.) He was born in Athens in 389 B.C. and died in Samos in 314, being self-exiled.

He was a powerful orator, a rival to Demosthenes. His parents were poor, but moral and honorable people. Because of this Aeschynes did not receive a philosophical education, but only in a practical way did he climb the levels of rhetorical art and evolved into a powerful and most well known orator, who played a significant role in the political life of Athens. In this his natural eloquence assisted and which, together with his imposing voice and his daring disposition, many times gave him the ability to improvise his orations.

In order to deal with the needs of life, Aeschynes worked at, different occupations early in life, such as, for example, that of the hypocrite, the actor and the author.

He owes his glory to the conflict he entered into with Demosthenes.

In 348 B.C. he appears for the first time in the political life of Athens and taking on an antimacedonian position, admonishes the Athenians to join together with the other cities against Philip (King of Macedonia – father of Alexander the Great (368-336 B.C.)

He fought in battles courageously against Philip and was crowned in battle (a great honor at that time) by the general Phokiona himself (he was chosen general 45 times, far surpassing Pericles' record, but he spent most of his life, 402-317 B.C., propagandizing the motto "No war.") But afterwards, however, he enters the pro Macedonian party.

Here we must note that at that time, there were two contesting parties.

- The antimacedonian (liberal) party with Demosthenes as head and
- The philirenic party (the philippizers) with Aeschynes as their head.

When Aeschynes, together with Demosthenes and other ambassadors, went to Macedonia to negotiate with Philip, his stance was favorable for the signing of Peace, which was called "Philocratean" (346 B.C.), Philocrates' name being used, who was its spokeman, because Philip succeeded in winning over Aeschynes completely with his persuasive nobility. At that time Aeschynes finally appears as a conscientious defender of an agreement between Athens and Macedonia and simuntaniously as an unrepentant rival of Demosthenes.

THE VIEWS OF THE TWO RIVALS

DEMOSTHENES: Philip has conquering inclinations and that is why Athens and the cities of southern Greece are in danger.
AESCHYNES: He supports Philip and assures the Athenians about the latters noble sentiments and his good dispositions towards the city and its allies.

After this (change of party of Aeschynes), Demosthenes,

- Did not for a moment stop his attacks against Philip in the Assembly of the Deme.
- Twice brought lawsuits against Aeschynes, with the unfounded accusation that he was bought off "taking Macedonian gold" from Philip and betrayed the interests of Athens. Demosthenes supported the accusation passionately, without, however, succeeding in achieving his condemnation, because Aeschynes in defending himself succeeded in proving that he was not guilty and was exonerated by a majority of 30 votes.

Thus from then on between the two orators began a destructive political and legal struggle.

Finally, however, Demosthenes' manly countenance and his eloquence which was full of patriotic eloquence, and Philip's forward advance towards the south, persuaded the Athenians to quickly organize an army and to march North, in order to deal with Philip's phalanxes. The murderous collision of the two armies occurred in 338 B.C. at Charoneia in Boetia, where Philip's army, being better organized and trained, completely defeated the unorganized army of the Athenians and the Thebeans, who fought having on there side the renowned Sacred Company.

The awarding of the historical crown of Greek Rhetoric, and the contest between the two orator-politicians, came in 330 B.C. Six years prior to this, the two implacable enemies, AESCHYNES, who was a simple and eloquent speaker, (Indeed it is said that he was the first Greek orator who spoke extemporaneously with great success, while his opponents wrote their speeches beforehand); and DEMOSTHENES, the father of Rhetoric, on the other hand, came into conflict, on the occasion of the proposition (he wrote a vote) of Ktesiphonta, who proposed to the appropriate advisor to award Demosthenes the gold crown in theater during the holiday of the great Dionysians, not only for his political orientation, but also for his many monetary offerings to the fatherland.

Aeschynes set himself against this proposal, which brought a lawsuit against Ktesiphonta, who criticized him of violating the laws. Thus was given him the opportunity to also directly attack the character and career of

Demosthenes. The latter, who had received the support of Ktesiphonta, answered the court with his famous speech "On Behalf of Ktesiphonta concerning Stephan."

Here we must note that each viewpoint of the two speeches at court is fought against with anger and possesses all the hatred that also characterizes two enemies who come against one another.

Demosthenes' speech was so powerful and passionately eloquent, that those under oath exonerated Ktesiphonta and condemned Aeschynes with a fine for slander and dishonor (a heavy punishment for that time), with five (5) votes in favor and one (1) against. It's indispensable for us to note that this trial was not a contest between these two orators, but in essence, between the two competing political parties, those for the Macedonians and the anti-macedonians, whose conflict would rage over for several decades, but the chief battles were between the two most powerful orators. The following year the Church of the Deme awarded the disputed gold crown to Demosthenes, and Aeschynes, because he could not pay the fine of 1000 drachmas that they fined him and having to deal with the vilification of losing his, exiled himself to Rhodes, where he lived a poor life, from the money he earned from teaching Rhetoric. From there he would leave Samos, where he also died in 314 B.C.

Aeschynes didn't leave us with a great work, perhaps because he had the ability to create extemporaneous speeches and it wasn't indispensable for him to write them down. Thus, from his speeches, only three were saved, which were delivered in courts, in which Demosthenes was adversary. These are: "Against Timarchos" in 346, "On the False Embassy" in 343 and "Against Ktesiphontas" in 330. All three of these speeches which Aeschynes delivered with much clarity, a thunderous voice and excellent acting, are, powerful and full of siginificant teachings. They left excellent impressions to subsequent specialists. The renowned Cicero translated the two, "Against Ktesiphontas" and "On the False Embassy." Finally, as is commonly confirmed, Aeschynes, whose speech was grandiose and graceful, was particularly distinguished for his genius and was Philip's most important supporter and Demosthenes' most brilliant opponent.

Some of his thoughts and views:

- He believed in the continual peace between the Athenians and the cities of southern Greece, along with Philip.
- He regarded Philip as a worthy and charismatic leader and believed that the union of Greek cities, which were constantly being run down by quarrels and civil wars, under the leadership of Philip, would create a better Greek region and perhaps a united Greece.

ARISTOTLE
(384-322 B.C.)

A famous philosopher who perfected ancient Greek Philosophy. He was born at Stagira of Macedonia in 384 B.C. and died in Chalkida in 322.

Aristotle was a great and systematic intellect. He dealt with practically all branches of science that were of interest to humanity. He was a genuine universal interpreter. His keen faculty of observing, his vast learning, and correct judgment made him into a chief exponent of Philosophy and Science.

In 368, at the age of 18, he went to Athens and entered Plato's Academy, where he would study beside his wise teacher, until his death, that is, in 347. During this 20 year period he studied Platonic philosophy and pre-Platonic Philosophy and set the foundations of his own Philosophy, initially with the creation of the Rhetorical School, which rivaled the School of Isocrates (436-338 B.C.)

After the death of his teacher, he immediately left from Athens and went to Asso of Asia Minor, where he remained for three years teaching. From there he left in 345 and settled in Mytilene, continuing his didactic and scientific work.

In 342 B.C. the King of Macedonia Philip invited him to Pella (an ancient capital of the Macedonians) and gave him the job of educationg Alexander, who was then 13 years old. Aristotle took pains so that Alexander would receive a good education and he especially initiated him in the Greek heroic tradition. The Homeric epics comprise the basis of his teaching.

Alexander appreciated Aristotle's efforts and the respect and love of the student towards his teacher is known. Indeed characteristic in this regard is that Alexander used to say that to Philip he owed life, and to Aristotle he owed the good life.

Aristotle in 335 left from Pella and settled in Athens, where he taught in a High School which was located on the shores of Ilissou. His School acquired great fame and was also called *peripatos* because of the great land that had stoae. For this and for the reason that Aristotle began to philosophize with his friends and taught his students as they were walking, his followers were called peripatetic Philosophers.

Aristotle taught and wrote for twelve years and whatever he succeeded in creating in this short time is worthy of great admiration, because he not only perfected and developed the philosophies of Socrates and Plato (he cared less for Plato is abstract approach and more for observation and experiment), but is also the founder of Positivism (Philosophy-Theory, according to which, only that which is perceived by the senses, exists) in Greek Philosophical and created the sciences of LOGIC, of PSYCHOLOGY, of PHYSICS, of METAPHYSICS, of Rhetoric etc.

Characteristic are his studies which he bequeathed to humanity concerning the Universe and its parts, concerning animate beings, the human being, ethics, virtue, politics, zoology, botany and music, which he distinguishes in a four-fold aspect, that is, game, moral formation (or cultivation), enjoyment, and catharsis. In his writings which were saved, there is stored knowledge which truly amazes one, for how was it possible for one man, and indeed in so short a time, to be able to collect such a great amount of knowledge and to structure it and organize it, alone, into a perfect philosophical system.

Concering his philosophy of life and the problems of human beings, and regarding the rules that must exist in the societal whole, he would say:

> *"Only those thoughts that guide to valuable actions are valuable. And happiness, the supreme good, is nothing other than the good and productive life, which is pervaded by correct laws. It is the function of ethics to provide these laws. The pleasures that engender within themselves a simple, egotistical satisfaction are completely bad. Some derive from the normal exercise of whatever capability, and, though they are not ends in themselves, are desirable. Even though prosperity, which contains within it health, wealth, friends and assists the family in the cultivation or formation of virtue – it is not however an essential element – a philosopher can draw power even from illness and poverty."* And he continues:
>
> *"No human being can live alone. True friendship, which engenders love for the good qualities that we discover in a friend and a selfless desire to be benefited by them, is one of the strongest moral powers in society. Thus, the more friendship spreads, the more it brings us towards the common life of society."*

Generous kings and rulers of Greece and of Asia and first of all Alexander the Great all marveled at his great genious, his unprecedented intellect and his irrepeatable activity. This, however, as occurs usually in such cases, provoked the envy of the contemporary Athenian philosophers, who in every way bitterly slandered and insulted him. He was accused, moreover, of being an atheist.

Tired, and above all, disgusted by the war that the Athenian philosophers and intellectuals of his time had declared, especially after the death of Alexander the Great, Aristotle, at the end of the summer of 323 B.C., took refuge in his mother's fatherland, Chalkida, where he also died, during the following summer and specificallly between July and September of 322, self-exiled and embittered (the penalty of truly great men...).

The body of the great philosopher was transferred from Chalkida to his birthplace city of Stagira. There his fellow citizens set up an altar, where the authorities of the city would hold conventions.

Fortunately, Diogenes Laertius (author 3rd century A.D.) refers to Aristotle's will, that irrepeatable great philosophical genius of antiquity, by whom we are informed of the brilliant and all-pure, we would say, character (gratitude, philanthropy, meekness, piety, etc.) of the Stagerite sage, upon whom so many sought to sling mud.

Some of his thoughts and views:

- The human being by nature is a social animal.
- The roots of paedia (education, culture, correct rearing) are bitter, but the fruits are sweet.
- Education requires three things: natural endowment, application to study, and exercises in the subject-matter.
- Those who carefully studied the manner of governance of peoples must have become convinced that the fortune of nations depends on the education of the youth.
- The purpose of the nation is not only the protection of the life and property of the citizens, but their being conducted to the highest point of moral and spiritual capability.
- We have a duty to consider God as an all-powerful spirit, immortal and perfect. For, though invisible to the eyes of people, He manifests himself by his works.
- The lower class revolts in order to become equal with all, and the equal class revolts in order to become superior. This is the mentality that creates revolutions.
- Poverty free from debt is great wealth.
- Justice, like every other virtue, is wisdom.
- Justice is virtue, according to which and according to the law, each person has whatever he or she needs to live.
- All virtues have their source in justice.
- There is no room in noble souls for hatred.
- Wherever there is a contest, there too is victory.
- Prudence is the mother and nurturer of every virtue.
- The laws that are rightly in force must foresee and anticipate all possible cases, as many as possible, so that they will leave the least possible number of laws in the judgment of the judges when they are trying cases.

DEMOSTHENES
(383-322 B.C.)

Demosthenes was the most famous orator of antiquity and of all time. He was born in Athens in 383 B.C. and died in Poros in 322.

From a youth he tasted the bitterness of life, because at the age of seven he became an orphan and his guardians and tutors misappropriated the property that his father had left him (who was a knife-maker and bed-maker in regard to occupation). Such was the indifference of the tutors towards the orphan that they even neglected his schooling. Besides this, the orphan had a few natural defects. He stammered (he had difficulty pronouncing the letters "l" and "r"), his breathing was weak and be could not say a single entire verse without interruption (without taking a breath, straight through). Moreover, he was physically ugly and sickly, and that's why he never attended the wrestling arena, as the youth of Athens were accustomed to doing. So he grew up in bad health, without socializing, apparently incapable of the active life and nurturing the desire to vindicate himself against those who had inflicted injustice upon him.

In order to achieve this and with the goal of serving his fatherland as a politician, Demosthenes with faith and patience succeeded in overcoming all his defects and he especially succeeded in governing his weak and defective voice by means of many years of training (tradition has it that he would at one time climb up the Lykabeto and at another time go down to Falero, in order to train his body and to deliver speeches by putting stones in his mouth) and prepared himself for his life as an orator.

The orator of this time would learn not only to invoke logic, but also to touch all the chords of human affection.

To the cheerful style of Lysias (orator 459-377 B.C.) and to the rational demonstration of Isaius (an orator of the time), he added a torrential surge that would completely dominate his listeners. He drew heavily from Thucydides' brain, from whom he drew knowledge about the past as well as his military ideal for the Nation. From Isaios and Isocrates and from others he took valuable lessons and studied speech delivery, having as a teacher a certain successful actor.

Behind this external equipment we discover his unsurpassed, peculiar genius and a fervent patriotism, which is combined with the religious zeal of a prophet; the practical politician who in his surge of eloquence never neglects showing the particular path towards happiness; the moral idealist, the leading defender of regional freedom against the intervening despotism of some high civilization against the evolution of some inferior civilization.

Though Demosthenes set himself against the events that helped the universalization of Hellenism, he at least enriched Hellenism with his superb rhetoric and even more with the manner in which he supported human freedom, which is the greatest gift of Greece to humanity.

Humanity will never stop marveling at the fervent patriotism of the man.

Demosthenes' unbridled political idiosyncracy, his genuine and flowing passion of rhetoric and his hyphestial personality were precisely what charmed certain great politicians of modern times.

On the assiduity and perfection of Demosthenes' speeches, the rhetoric teacher Kointilianos will say:

> *"So much power exists in him, so concentrated is everything, so full of internal intensity, so carefully thought out, structured and organized, such orderliness exists in the discourse, that you cannot even discover anything missing, nor anything that is superfluous."*

As an advocate at the courts, he had many clients, as the discourses he wrote until 345 indicate. But he obtained his most significant fame by means of his political speeches to the Athenians, beginning at the age of 29, in which he advises, demonstrates, foretells and forewarns, admonishes and indicts.

His speeches against King Philip ("The Philippic Speeches") who, taking advantage of a weak and irregular situation that was then prevailing in Athens, aimed at governing throughout all Greece, are truly monumental discourses and unmatched examples of courage, patriotism, and love for freedom.

At that time, the common opinion of Athens was divided into two parties. The first was indifferent and perhaps viewed Philips plans favorably (Phocas, Isocrates); and the second, the so-called antimacedonian party, whose head was Demosthenes, obstinately and with fierce militancy battled against the plans and the visions of Philip.

Demosthenes would attempt, with his discourses filled with unrelenting hatred against Philip's to raise the morale of the Athenians which had been relaxed completely during that time and a large portion of the citizens was indifferent about the visions and actions of Philip. Thus, he began to pressure his compatriots to sacrifice themselves and to suffer in behalf of their fatherland.

In the first Philipic, which was delivered in 351 B.C., he said to the Athenians that Philip had become great and powerful because of their inertia, and that if they were planning on stopping him, they would have to maintain a fleet in the Northern Aegean. They would also have to enlist many men in the army and the rich ought to pay for the costs. But Demosthenes was still young and his words didn't carry much weight.

With his third Philippic – a significant discourse – he greatly aroused Athens, in order to deal with the danger that was threatening the city due to

Philip. With his rhetorical power and with his presence in Thebes, he succeeded not only in persuading the Athenians to fight against Philip, but to unite with the up until then enemy cities and to align themselves together against Philip in Cheronea (338), where Philip was victorious after a murderous battle (Demosthenes took part as a simple soldier). After that defeat, the Athenians relegated to him the task of delivering the funeral oration speech for those fallen in battle.

Here we will have to note that Demosthenes would see the struggle between Greece and Macedonia as a war between free nations fought in a primitive land which was ruled by an autocratic King. That is to say, Demosthenes sees the struggle of the Athenians against Philip as the struggle of the State against the Monarchy. In other words, the struggle of the free nation that is governed according to laws, against the arbitrary authority of a single person.

The struggle for this idea which Demosthenes undertook with all the strength of his flaming soul, sets him very high above the circle of the usual demagogues because is orator had a political ideal: he became consumed in this struggle and that's why he devoted himself with fiery fanaticism to the great political mission of his fatherland city.

After the death of Philip, Demosthenes continued his struggle also against Alexander and admonished the Greek cities to offer resistance against the young king, without, however, any success. But when Alexander strictly punished Thebes with general destruction and prevailed fully in the Greek region, the voice of the orator became silent. Moreover, at trial, for the stealing of the treasures-spoils of Alexander, he was accused of corrupting the conscience of a judge or witness (bribery), and, not being able to pay the fine, which they set, he was jailed, only for him to escape with the help of his admirers and friends and to go to Aegina and to Troezen, from where he didn't stop rousing different Greek cities to take up arms against the invading Macedonians.

After the death of Alexander in Asia (Babylonia, June 11, 323 B.C., at the age only of 33 years old, after reigning for 13 years), the deme voted for the return of Demosthenes to Athens. But again too, after the new defeat of the Greeks in Cratona, the Macedonian victor Antipater, asked for the orator to be condemned to death. Demosthenes being persecuted took refuge in the temple of Poseidon and expired in front of the altar, in October of 322.

Forty years, after his tragic death, the Athenians set up a bronze statue of Demosthenes in the agora, on the basis of which was inscribed the epigram:

> *"Demosthenes, if you had power equal to your opinion, the Greek Macedonian Ares (Philip) would not have dominated the Greeks."*

Demosthenes wrote many discourses, but only 61 were saved, that is:

- 14 speeches to the deme, of which 11 are called four Philipic discourses these four are entitled "Against Philip" and they were delivered, the first in 351, the second in 344, the third and fourth in 341 and three are entitled *Olynthiac* which were delivered in 349 and 348 and had as content the helping and saving of Olynthos (and ancient Greek city in Chalkidiki) from the danger of Philip. The *Olynthiac* addresses are brief, but are excellent creations of his powerful artistry.
- 13 public forensic speeches (addresses before a court) and
- 34 private speeches.

The four Philippic discourses and the three *Olynthiac* ones made him most worthy to the Athenians and rendered him immortal, because he worked at these fiery speeches of his painstakingly hard and to the minutest detail.

Some of his thoughts and views:

- It is more difficult to guard your goods than to gain them.
- Money then is necessary, and nothing that needs to be done can be done without it.
- It's better for one to be a begger than to be uneducated.
- What is a friend? One soul in two bodies.
- O mortal and miserable race! We are but a shadow and nothing else.
- The more capable one is, the more dangerous one is to society if one makes bad use of one's capability.
- The dead share no more in goods; however, the praises for whatever good actions they might have done belong to them, and this possession of theirs is inalienable. And this is so because envy has already stopped combating them.
- The only consolation that sweetens the unfortunate ones is the thought that they have fulfilled their duty.
- Don't choose the life of a rabbit (a coward).
- It is not possible for one human being to do everything.

LYCURGUS THE ATHENIAN
(?-324 B.C.)

Lycurgus was a politician and orator. He was born in Athens, unknown when, and died there in 324 B.C.

He was a significant political figure and aligned himself with Demosthenes in the endeavor aiming at the administrative restoration of Athens.

The education that the charismatic youth received was excellent because he was fortunate enough to have Isocrates and Plato as teachers.

Lycurgus, who had succeeded Demosthenes as leader of the democrats, devoted, after the battle of Cheronias in 338 B.C. (at the end of this section a few words about the battle will be said), all his activity for the restoration of Athens, so that with the passing of time, the city would be able to take the place it deserves, that is, the rulership of Greece.

He was elected Treasurer (an institution that was established from the time of Cleisthenes. The treasurers who were of different categories, were economic rulers, who had as their job the handling of the public or private interests) of the city for 15 or 12 years. Here it is worth noting that the institution of Treasurer was also the first step towards the unification of public funds. Lycurgus' regime was one of the most significant in the history of Athens and this was so because he succeeded in realizing many significant material and spiritual works in it, as, for example:

- He adorned Athens with statues of many distinguished artists and generally gave much care to the beautification of the citymore so than anyone after Pericles.
- The great theater of Dionysus was built again with stone.
- He restored the walls.
- He completed the renowned for his time ship building of Philona at Pireas.
- He built the stadium of Ilisos, Odeo, and the High School Gymnasium (the famous gymnasium at Ilisos.)

These edifices could be completed only with prudence and the strict handling of funds. This tactical and cautious handling of funds, combined with increased income, also provided Athens with the possibility of simultaneously reorganizing military resources. We should mention that Lycurgus was not only a good orator, but also a very good economist. We could easily describe him as being a modern financial expert and indeed a successful one at that.

His politics were at bottom antimacedonian, (at that time the Athenians, but even practically all the Greeks, were divided into two political parties: The one in favor of Philip, with Aeschynes as head, and the other against Philip, having Demosthenes as head) and he envisioned the resurrection of ancient Athens, which, with its military and spiritual power would be able to again become the center of the world.

For one to achieve the above two aims, Lycurgus:

- developed such cultural and embellishing activity, that this was the reason why he was compared by many with Pericles himself in the area of constructing beautiful buildings.
- as Treasurer of the city of Athens he followed a virtuous political line, combining it with the establishment of various restorative laws.
- published the works of great tragic poets, Aeschylus, Sophocles and Euripides, looking toward the development and cultivation of the spiritual level of the people.
- In the military sphere, he not only enlarged the fleet (400 triremes), but he also changed legislation regarding the youth, who now were obligated by the age of 19 and 20 years old to pass a year in military education and a second year in guard service at the borders.

With the above two visible and effective actions, the Athenian nation, truly, again found its power with a very swift pace and the people, on whom Lycurgus supported himself, appeared satisfied by his political stance.

Lycurgus died in 324 B.C. and is considered one of the last noble figures of the ancient Greek world, who struggled for his sublime ideals.

The Athenians appreciated his valuable offering to the city, as well as his diamond-like character, and for this reason they honored Lycurgus with a bronze statue (307 B.C.) and they ceded to a large number of his descendents the right to eat at the Prytaneum.

The PRYTANEUM was the archive of every ancient Greek city. At Athens it was one of the most significant buildings of the Agora ("market-place") and it was located at the Southern side of the Acropolis. At the Prytaneum there were statues of Peace and Estia, the Unextinguished Fire of the city and the Laws of Solon. There were given the honorary dinners to foreign embassadors and to distinguished citizens. At the Prytaneum there remained also the named Ruler and trials were held for murders with unknown perpetrators.

THE BATTLE AT CHERONEA

Cheronea was a historical city of Boetia, near today's Levadia. There in 338 B.C. a harsh and decisive battle was fought between the Macedonians and the army of the antimacedonian alliance, having the Athenians and the Thebans at their head. In this battle the son of Philip, Alexander, took part, who then was only 18 years old, leading two thousand horsemen. The Sacred Company of the Thebans faught the Macedonians, the former being the famous military unit which was comprised of the best fighters of Boetia, who had sworn: "Never retreat, death on the battle ground." The Macedonian army, better organized, being disciplined, and especially with a worthy leadership, having defeated the Sacred Company, had annihilated in a few hours all the allied powers of Greece. The Athenians and the Thebans, exceptionally honored their dead at the battle of Cheronia. Indeed, they latter built an empty tomb, on which they set a marble lion, the well-known Lion of Cheronea.

Philip's victory at Cheronea constitutes a significant event for the history of Ancient Greece and it encapsulated two basic events:

- It would now distinguish Philip undoubtedly as the leader of the Panhellenic Political Union and
- Essentially it marked the death of the City-State, which for years comprised the core of the political constitution in the Hellenic region, and in which very often ambitions created friction between cities and bloody wars.

THEOPHRASTUS
(372-287 B.C.)

Theophrastus was an ancient Greek philospher, a student and successor of Aristotle at the School.

He was born in Eresso of Lesbos. His initial name was Tyrtamos, but for the "Grace of his language," Aristotle (384-332 B.C.) changed his name to THEOPHRASTON.

After Aristotle's departure from Chalkida, he took on the administration of the School, which he maintained for 34 years, that is, from 322 until his death in 287.

As the more than 2,000 of his students testify, among them the comic Menandros (342-290 B.C.) he had the gift of speech. His students particularly loved this eloquent philosopher and even foreign rulers honored him with exceptional honors, as, for example, Cassandros (King of Macedonia 350-298 B.C.) and Ptolemy (King of Egypt). The love of the Athenians was so great and especially sincere, that when Agnonides (an Athenian demagogue of the 4th century B.C.) dared to write impiously against him, they all rose up as in one body against him and he was in danger of being condemned as a slanderer.

The philosopher was not distinguished only for his excellent manner of instruction, but also for his wealthy production of writings.

Diogenes Laertius (a Greek author of the 3rd century A.D.) mentions more than 200 writings of his, but up to our day, except for many fragments, there have survived complete the following:

- A literary piece entitled "Characters," which is comprised of 30 chapters, where the philosopher, laconically, but with great clarity represents human characters in society and
- Two valuable botanical writings, that is:
  "Botanical Histories," which consists of nine books and describes plants and "Causes of Plants" which consists of six books and refers to the theoretical part of Botanical Science.

Both examine, in detail, the world of plants and present a significant amount of knowledge concerning plants for that time.

The study of plants was begun by Aristotle and THEOPHRASTUS continued it, developed it, and finally published it.

Thus, in this branch, the student, surpassed his teacher, and for this reason he is justly recognized as the father of Botany.

Besides the above, he distinguishes one more significant work of THEOPHRASTUS: "On Stones" which is a fragment of the great work, which had as its subject Minerology. From this fragment we draw knowledge about how the ancients cut stones and fashioned them.

The surviving works of THEOPHRASTUS were published for the first time at Venetia in 1497.

Some thoughts and views of his:

- Virtuous people have need of very few laws.
- The envious ones are not pleased so much about their own blessings as much as they are about the disasters that befall others.
- Ingratitude is the betrayal of humanity.
- Beauty is a silent deception.
- Cowardliness is a movement of the soul that advances or retreats before a real or imagined danger.
- Flattery is a shameful form of merchandizing from which only the flatterer comes out winning.
- The prudent must never do anything when they are found in a state of wrath.
- One is the principle, that is, one is the Being, and that is everything…because that which is found within it is everything, is God: this “wholistic being” is neither limited, nor infinite, nor moves, nor remains still.

PHILEMON
(361-261? B.C.)

Philemon was a noteworthy poet of the so-called New Comedy. He was born in Syracuse (an ancient Greek city of Sicily) about 361 B.C. and died within the ten-year period of 260.

Before 307 B.C. he became an Athenian citizen.

In his long life – he lived about 100 years – he wrote 97 comedies, of which 60 titles survive.

His first victory was marked at the Dionysia in 327 B.C. (a feast-day celebration held in honor of Dionysus, god of wine and vineyards).

He won three times at Lenea and in the list of victors he would come in immediately after Menander (348-290 B.C.), together with whom they comprised at this time the gigh point of theatrical art.

It is worth mentioning that Philemon maintained all his bodily and spiritual capabilities up until his death, which some attribute to his excessive laughter, while others mention that he died reading a book. Whichever view we consider, the truth is one: he abandoned worldy things being happy, with a shaking laugh or with a spiritual intensity and yearning.

His most significant works were "Emporoi," "Thesauros" and "Phasma." And he possessed marvelous capablity in the art of drama.

Some of his thoughts and views:

- It is better to die than to live miserably.
- The just person is not one who does not inflict injustice, but one who, though capable of inflicting injustice, does not want to.
- You are a human being – know this and always remember it.
- Sorrow is a tree whose fruit is tears.
- Believe that God exists and worship him but don't search about to find him, because you won't achieve anything else than getting tired of searching.
- Constrained anger is characteristic of the prudent.
- The passions are not capable of being uprooted. For this reason it is necessary that each person satisfies them within the bounds of virtue.
- If tears were a medicine for our pains, crying would be cured once and for all and we would even purchase tears by giving gold.
- Even if you are a slave, you are no less a human being, if you are a human being.
- It is difficult to execute, but easy to command.
- Whichever arts have evolved, they were taught by time, not by a teacher.

ERASISTRATUS
(3RD century B.C.)

Erasistratus was the greatest Naturalist of antiquity. He was born on the island of Kea, unknown when. He studied at Athens and practiced Medicine in Alexandria, about 258 B.C. He made a clearer distinction than Erophilos between the brain and the cerebellum, and performed experiments on animals, in order to study the function of the brain. He described and explained the function of the epiglottis, the lymphatic vessels of the mesentery, as well as the aorta and heart valves. Every organ, Erasistratus would say, is conjoined to the rest of the organism in three ways: by arteries, veins and nerves. He attempted to explain all physiological phenomena by means of physical causes, rejecting every mystical explanation. He understood the art of Medicine to be preventative, placing a greater emphasis on hygiene than on therapy. For this reason he didn't recommend the frequent use of medicine and he recommended diet, baths and physical exercises. At that time many cities had public medical service, in which doctors received a small fee, but enjoyed a particular admiration among the people, because they didn't make a distinction between rich and poor, free people and slaves, and were devoted constantly and exclusively to their work. Thus, they held high the tradition that they had received as a valuable inheritance from Hippocrates.

MENANDER
(342-290 B.C.)

Menander was a most prominent Athenian comedian of the so-called New Attic School. He was born in 342 B.C. in Athens, where he lived and died in 290.

He was nephew to the comedy writer Alexidus and clarify Theophrastus (a philosopher from Lesbos 372-287 B.C.)

His first work entitiled "Wrath" was performed in 324 and in 316 it won in the theater competitions. From then on he won another seven times, even though he wrote a large number of works.

Menander drew great attention, because he depicted sympathetic characters in arguments and gives a vivid and variegated representation of daily life, a real image of difficulties experienced in households, but having a happy resolution.

The plot of his work "Allowing," as well as his other works, have to do with separated families who meet again at the end, after some scene involving recognition, but the atmosphere, the circumstances, and the main features are different each time.

Menander exercised great influence on following centuries and especially since Roman times, in which Plautus* and especially Terence** imitated him or presented, in their works, his works paraphrased, until the time of Shakespeare.

The number of his works reached more than 100. Unfortunately, however, no comedy of his has survived, except for large fragments.

Of his works the following comedies stand out the most:

- *Epitrepontes*, where the poet touches upon, among other things, a significant social issue of the time, the issue of "exposing" (that is, the placing of a child outside, which its parents secretly abandoned), which was dealt with earlier by Plato and Aristotle.
- *Samia*, in which, chiefly, two neighboring families are presented, the family of the wealthy Demea and of the poor Nicaretus, whose children fall in love and the known, unacceptable family problems, which are also known today, are created.
- *Perikeiromeni* has as subject two exposed twin children (one male one female) of the daughter of the merchant Pataicus.

As we also see in this comedy, he would examine the social wound of that time, that is, the great problem of the exposition of infants, which also

* A Roman comedian.

** A Roman writer of comedies.

occupies today's global society, except not as intensely, because there are manners of dealing with the problem by means of the existence of various institutions and social services.

It should be stated here that in 1907, papyroi began to be found in the sands of Egypt that had great excerpts from the comedies of Menander, and thus we now have very great portions of his aforementioned comedies. Moreover, there were also found some verses of his other comedies, of "Farmer," "Flatterer," "Kitharistou" and "Hero."

From the above it seems that Menander was:

- A man with deep humanistic feelings and a rich psychical world, which surely prompted him to deal with the issue of the human being and to present daily persons, family and social problems, would the hope that this will contribute to their reduction if not in their solution.
- A poet of great talent, who was appreciated not only by his contemporary spiritual people, but by later ones as well. This is, after all, also proved by the fact that Cicero marveled at him and particularly praised him.

Some of his thoughts and views:

- Greediness is the greatest evil among people.
- Whoever is loved by the gods dies young.
- The doctor of all necessary evils is time.
- Above all things look to honor your parents.
- How happy is the human being when he or she is a human being.
- Don't hold perpetual enmity. Reflect that you are mortal.
- Instead of saying "know thyself," it would be better to say many times "know the others."
- In telling the truth, you choose the best method and the most secure manner for living the best life.
- The temple of God is found everywhere, if only we seek it out with our thought and our prayer.
- Wisdom is an asset much more valuable than wealth.
- Peace nurtures even the farmer's stones, while war destroys even the land.
- Education is an inalienable right of people.
- Don't wait first to be punished in order to learn the law, but preventively anticipate punishment by your respect towards it.
- The uneducated person is brazen.
- The only person among people that is rich is the person who is self-sufficient.

- Wealth covers over many evil actions.
- Only silence doesn't make you repent.
- It seems to me that the person who blushes is a good person.
- A person must at every moment be ready for every contingency of life, because nothing in it is stable and durable.
- When a law is kept, it is only law. However, when it is violated it is both law and executioner.
- All the animals are happier than the human being, because they don't have mind.
- Envy is the worst evil of all, because it corrupts the person who has it.

EPICURUS
(341-270 B.C.)

A famous materialist philosopher of antiquity, who influenced Greek thought with his teaching. He was born in 341 B.C. in Samos, from Athenian parents (his father was a poor possessor by allotment) and he died in Athens in 270, at the age of 72. He learned his encyclopedic letters in the city of Teos, where, perhaps, for the first time he was taught Mathematics and the Natural Philosophy of the Ionians. An intelligent mind, he plunged into study and became cultivated as did few in his time. As Diogenes Laertius (a Greek author of the 3rd century A.D.) informs us, he zealously applied himself to the Philosophy of Democritus, the Dialogues of Plato, as well as the Writings of Aristotle. Epicurus, in his formulation of his philosophical system, worked with vigor toward self-perfection, without faithfully following any foreign teaching and theory. Of course, he took much from the Physics of Democritus; he is not, however, a simple copyist, as many of the ancients believe, as well as many modern historians of Philosophy.

He taught at Lampsako (an ancient city at the Hellespont) and in Mytilene, where he opened his School. His students were many and his teaching made a big impact (310). Later they called him to Athens and gave him a house and a small garden. He accepted the invitation and in 306, that is, at the age of 35, he came and established the School. In the Garden, the new philosopher would gather together many students. He was a philosopher who preached new dogmas. He continued where Democritus left off and popularized the latter's philosophy, whom, however, he did not follow in every respect, but made complementary additions to his Materialistic Philosophy.

Epicurus is one of the three great Thinkers of antiquity (Democritus, Epicurus, Lucretius) and his School, like the Stoic stoa, was Materialistic and essentially accepted the atomic theory of Democritus. Even the soul, he held, is material and is dissolved at death. Since it is mortal, we have nothing to fear from some future life. Gods exist, but not those of the popular faith. The real divinities don't have any relation with the world and live separately from it with cloudless happiness, without, however, caring at all about the human race.

The protarchic pleasure and the basis of all hedonistic feelings is, according to the teaching of Epicurus, bodily pleasure, that is, the enjoyment of the senses. It is understood that Epicurus wasn't giving his teaching vulgar content. On the contrary, he wanted to apply the brakes on the unbridled debauchery of the people of his time. And for this reason he taught that the greatest good is to be found in psychical pleasure:

> *"The sensual pleasures are quick and transient, while those of the spirit are superb and constant. For this reason the prudent person will*

choose poverty and bodily sufferings, if he or she is to secure the greatest pleasures."

The supreme good, just as with the Stoics, is HAPPINESS. But for Epicurus, happiness is the liberation from pain or fear which constitutes intellectual suffering. That is to say, that happiness and pain are two poles around which revolve the alternating life of people.

Here it is also worth mentioning another basic aim of Epicurus' theory, which was the pursuit of HESYCHIA, that is, quietude, stillness. And this was so because he lived at the time of Greece's decline (the Greek cities would underwent a great crisis and in parallel course many great and unsolvable problems were being created), the characteristic of which is political fatigue – do you see how far back the roots of our soul have their source? – He propagandized the idea of friendship and lack of perturbation. He used to say that for people to achieve this calmness, they must abstain from politics (a prophetic problem for modern Greeks), you must – he stressed – be freed from the slavery of the bonds of vain things and of politics and to indispensably "Live in obscurity."

And he moreover taught abstention from political activity: "Don't participate in common affairs."

Epicurus possessed an intelligent and most admirable character. He passionately loved work and his exclusive, objective goal was to benefit his fellow human beings. According to Cicero he was renowned for his philanthropic actions.

The result of the great love that he had for his work was the creation of many works, which included 300 cylinders (volumes). Of these, as Diogenes Laertius informs us is a work entitled *On Nature*, 44 ethical opinions, three letters, that is, *To Herodotus*, which contains the primary principles of the Epicurian system, *To Pythocles*, which refers to meteorological phenomena and *To Menoeceus*, wherein he sets forth his moral theories, which also constituted the breath of his life, in such a way, that these would be disseminated beyond the circle of his students:

- "On the End" (concerning the highest purpose of life).
- "On Lives" (paths of life).
- "On what to prefer and what to avoid." (What we must do and what we must not do).

Finally, we must mention that the human being comprised the utmost importance for this system. In contrast to the stoic, the follower of Epicurus doesn't nurture any spiritual ideal for which to struggle.

It is true, that this system, as it was initially taught, created several exceptionally worthy characters. But the general result was corruptive. For, they very willingly perverted the dogma of happiness and Epicurus' philosophy became synonymous with the love of food and drink, with gluttony and the most crude forms of pleasure.

Epicurus died in 270 at the age of 72 years old and left behind many students and admirers. No other ancient Philosophical School acquired so many followers and students, or lasted for so many years.

Some of his thoughts and views:

- Philosophy, and generally every form of knowledge, is a basic source of human happiness.
- Physics is needed only because the knowledge we acquire from it liberates us from the fear of the gods, death and punishment after death etc.
- The only principle of things is matter, and outside of matter there is nothing other than a void.
- Morality is the highest good, but the only means to achieve it is by means of the greater good, that is, to live very pleasantly, which is impossible to achieve without living with prudence, goodness, and justice.
- The only absolute good is "pleasure," not momentary pleasure however, but constant pleasure, and the only absolute evil is pain, sorrow.
- Bravo to nature! It made necessary things easily obtainable and things not necessary difficult to obtain.
- If you want to make someone rich, don't add money to him, but subtract his desires.
- Death is nothing for us. For he who died doesn't feel or sense anything, and what is without sense does not concern us.
- While we are living, death is not present. When he appears, then we aren't alive.
- One cannot live pleasantly without living prudently, well and righteously. Nor can one live prudently, well, and righteously, without living pleasantly.
- Now virtue is nothing else than rational prudence, leading the prudent person by means of pleasure to the happy life.
- When legislation does not look to the interest of society, it never possesses the character of just legislation.

MENECRATES THE SAMIAN

- Though each person wishes to reach a long old age, when they reach old age they complain and slander.
- If a person who has grown old wishes to live longer, he or she is worthy of living as an old person for a few more decades.
- Quit yourself from oaths, if you can, always, or as much as possible.

ZENO THE CITIEUS
(336-238 B.C.)

Zeno was a Greek philosopher, the founder of Stoic Philosophy, and a contemporary of Epicurus (a Greek philosopher from Samos 341-270 B.C.)

Little is known about his life. He was born in Kitio of Cyprus and went to Athens in 315 B.C., where he founded the Stoic School. (310). There, for a sufficient length of time, he studied with the cynics, but he simultaneously also attended the teaching of Xenocrates (a philosopher from Chalcedon 396-314 B.C.).

A few years later he began to teach independently and to develop his own theories, at the "Poikili Stoa," which gave its name to his School.

Zeno tirelessly taught for a half a century and up until his death. Many of his students followed his example, that is, those who particularly loved and admired him.

He wrote many works, but they were all lost.

His character was dispassionate, unperturbed, and calm, and his life was generally a brilliant example for imitation. For this reason, but also for his most interesting and humane philosophy, the Athenians honored him both while he was alive as well as when he was dead, by erecting a monument whose epigraph read that the life of the philosopher was completely in with his teachings.

Zeno lived as a hermit and usually ate bread, honey and figs. He only drank water.

The central idea of Zeno's theory was the formation of a person's character, so that he or she could deal with the difficulties of life (in the world).

He believed that humanity needed greater individual self-sufficeincy and taught that, in order for one to achieve this aim, it is necessary for one to exercise one's will and to become partners with Nature, to desire only those things that one is certain will be realized by means of one's will. In order to prove that this central dogma is logical and that one will thereby achieve happiness, Zeno developed an entire philosophical system, which is comprised of three branches:

- LOGIC, in which he develops a theory of knowledge.
- PHYSICS, which deals with the study of Nature and of which the most amazing principle is that everything is material, even God and the human soul.
- ETHICS, in which, among other things, he taught:

Everything in Nature is rational and good. Thus, from *physics* we pass on unawares to *ethics*. The soul of the human being is part of the divine soul and the virtuous life is signifies a partnership with Nature. Everything that exists is beneficial for the human being, even sickness, the harmful animals, earthquakes and other such things: these things are preordained for our training. In this way, we are gradually led back to the central idea of stoicism, namely, that we reach HAPPINESS, which is the supreme good, when we make our will to enter into partnership with the laws of nature, which are absolutely rational and just.

With Zeno and his successors Stoicism became a religion, which had at its base the entering of the human will into partnership with Nature, which is nothing more than the subjection to the will of God. This is pure monotheism, the worship of the Supreme Being. Since He only wants our good, and blesses, yet He never harms us. We, who comprise parts of Him, have no reason to fear Him, but only to respect and love Him.

This form of worship has no need of altars or temples or icons or even of prayers, but only of purity in thought and life.

Some of his thoughts and views:

- The life according to nature is the life according to virtue.
- The cities must not be adorned with objects of dedication, but with the virtues of its inhabitants.
- Nature gave us one tongue and two ears, so that we can listen twice as much as what we speak.

CLEANTHES
(331-232 B.C.)

Cleanthes was a stoic philosopher and successor of Zeno at the School of the Stoa. He was born in the city of Asso of Troada (the land of Troy) in 331 B.C. and lived in Athens where he died (he went on a hunger strike, in order to end his bodily illness), in deep old age, in the year 232, that is, at the age of 99.

It is said he was a boxer and that when he reached Athens, all his assets consisted of four drachmas. But his desire and zeal for philosophical studies was so great, that, in order to cover his costs and to attend Zeno's instruction, he would draw water and sprinkle gardens all night. That's why they teasingly called him "Well-drawer." A characteristic mark of his poverty was the fact that, in order to secure his bread, he would grind wheat on the stone hand-mill of a bakery.

Cleanthes was exceptionally robust. He lived with strict frugality, as a hermit and would eat bread, honey and figs, like his teacher.

Though brought from a foreign land of unknown origin, he won the respect and admiration of the Athenians with his virtue and his exemplary asceticism. Zeno admired him particularly and considered him his most faithful and virtuous student. Here it is worth mentioning that Cleanthes quickly assimilated philosophical thoughts and ideas, but, though quick in the apprehension of ideas, was deep in his thought. To the frequent teasings of others he responded with coolness, readiness, goodness and special grace. It is said that his fellow students called him "Mule." And he, jestingly would answer: "Yes, that's why perhaps I'm the only one who can carry Zeno's burden." He studied for 19 years at the Stoic school and when its leader died, he was judged to be the only person worthy to succeed Zeno at the Acholl, where he remained until his death, completing in many respects the teachings of the Stoa's Founder.

With Cleanthes and the other successors of Zeno Stoicism became a religion. Here are some of its theoretical thoughts:

- "The only motive for correct behavior, the partnership with nature, is nothing more than the subjection to the will of god." This is pure monotheism, the worship of the Supreme Being.
- Since He only wants our good, and blessing, yet He never harms us. We who comprise parts of Him, have no reason to fear Him, but only to respect and love Him.

From the teaching of Zeno and his successors comes the conclusion that they recognized equality between free persons and slaves, between Greeks and Barbarians. The old dogma *"every non-Greek is a barbarian"* is no longer heard or at least doesn't hold sway among the large strata of the population.

It was natural for the above views to be formulated, because the basis of Stoic philosophy, which looks to the formation of the human beings' character, is the teaching concerning virtue, which must be people's unique aim.

- "All material and moral benefits (wealth, offices, health, etc.) are of no absolutely benefit without virtue."
- "Virtue is the perfect good, the aim of human activity."

Cleanthes' teaching was not very charming, because he was somewhat deficient in oral speech, though as an author and poet he had many gifts, as the marvelous hymn to Zeus testifies, (which has fully survived), as well as other fragments from various but philosophical poems. The "Hymn to Zeus" has survived due to Stobaios and contains the chief elements of his philosophy and particularly his moral teaching, as, for example:

- The self-willed conducting of the individual volition to the law that pervades the Universe is virtue and wisdom.
- "Neither is pleasure good, nor pain evil."
- "The supreme good is to live according to nature."
- "We have our origin from you."
- "No work is done on earth without you."

Diogenes Laertius (a Greek author of the 3rd century A.D.), in one of his lists, presents us with 50 titles of works of Cleanthes, in which he treats of subjects concerning natural, moral, and logical issues, of which, unfortunately, only a few small fragments have survived.

The works and days of the philosopher were a brilliant example for imitation. This, combined with his heavy philosophical work, helped to make his memory to be so revered that the Romans, after his death, set up his statue at the city of his birthplace in Asso.

Some of his thoughts and views:

- The soul suffers together with the body when it is ill, and the body suffers with the soul.
- The greatest good is to live truly in accord with nature.
- The uneducated differ only in form from the beasts.
- Ruler of nature, who rules all things by law.

EUCLID
(330-275 or 270 B.C.)

Euclid was a great Greek geometrician of antiquity. He is more ancient than Eratosthenes and Archimedes.

Regarding his life we have little information. Thus, we do not know with certainty where he was born. Many consider him a Sicilian. But Arabic sources mention that he was born in the city of Turo in Syria. Moreover, we don't know who his teachers were, and this is why they often identify him, in different editions, with the philosopher Socrates' student, Euclid the Megarean.

The broadness of his spirit and his excellent progress in his mathematical works quickly made him known, not only in the Greek region, but also in the outside world. Thus, he was invited to Alexandria by Ptolemy I in order to teach at its Museum, where he founded the famous Mathematical School of Alexandria.

His teaching and proficiency in Geometry were so amazing that his name became identified with the idea of Geometry, resulting in his contemporaries and subsequent generations until the Middle Ages remaining ignorant of Euclid's existence, thinking that his name was some significant point (key) of Geometry. Plus they considered the author of his most important work to be Theonas, Hypatias' father.

Euclid was calm, sweet in his behavior, and his modesty and ethos left behind a legacy.

Proclus (a neoplatonic philosopher) mentions that, when at one time Ptolemy asked Euclid if he could learn Geometry without laboring, he responded with the memorable: "There is no royal path to Geometry."

Euclid was an idealist and for this reason he believed that one must acquire knowledge of geometry for its own sake and not to secure some material (economic) profit.

He is the first founder of "axioms" as, for example: "From a point found outside a line is created a parallel line, and only a single parallel line. And the sum total of the three angles for all triangles is equal to two right angles."

He wrote many works, but his monumental work is "Elements," ("Stoicheia") from which he was called "Stoicheiotou" ("Elementator"). This work contains the primary propostions of Elemental Geometry and the theory of numbers and is divided into 13 books, that is:

- The six first ones deal with plane geometry.
- The seventh until the tenth treats of Arithmetic and
- The three last ones deal with stereometry.

The "Elements" are not a work of Euclid. On the contrary, entire books have been taken from his predecessors (Pythagoras, Hippicrates the Chian, Evdoxus the Knidian etc.)

The significance of the "Elements" and their influence in the teaching of Geometry was very great. Thus, the "Elements" comprised the main instructional book, from it authorship until, almost, our own days. They were translated into Arabic in the ninth century A.D., and also into Persian and Latin, from which they also became known also in Europe.

The first Greek text was published in the Kingdom of Switzerland in 1553.

Apart from the "Elements" there are saved also the following works of his: *Dethomena*, *Optica*, *Katoptrika*, *On Division*, and the *Phenomena*.

Some of his thoughts and views:

- A point is not a part of space.
- There is no royal path to Geometry. (His response to Ptolemy, who had asked him if he could learn Geometry without laboring).
- Euclid's palm is empty of coins. (Another response of the idealist Euclid to the same King).

ARISTARCHUS

Aristarchus was a famous astronomer of antiquity. He was born in Samos in 320 B.C. He lived in Samos, Athens, Alexandria and Lampsako (an ancient city on the Hellespont), where it is said that he died in 250.

As a youth he went to Athens, which was the greatest spiritual center of that time. In Athens he was taught many things near by great philosopher of his time, Stratona, who had succeeded Theophrastus as dean of the Aristotelian School.

His love and zeal for learning, especially for astronomy, was so great, that he studied with marvelous patience and interest all its branches which resulted in his distinction in all of these areas.

During his sojourn in Athens he formulated, as it is said, his helio-centric theory. With this theory, Aristarchus accepts the idea that the center of the cosmos (Universe) is the Sun and that the Earth revolves around it, while simultaneously revolving around its axis. So he is the first to teach that Earth "revolves around the Sun" and the first who theoretically formulated the astronomical theory of heliocentricism.

On this subject Archimedes, in his work "Psamittes," categorically attributes to Aristarchus the hypothesis that the fixed stars and the Sun remain unmoved and that the Sun is found in the middle of the orbit." Concerning the same subject Plutarch also should have been condemned, because he "set the Estia of the Cosmos (Universe), that is, the Earth into movement." Consequently, Aristarchus is justly regarded as being the Copernicus of antiquity.

However, the Athenian citizens were not sufficiently mature to accept his ideas, and they conedemned him for atheism, after a charge brought against him by Cleanthes, for "moving the seat of the universe and agitating the tranquility of the Olympian gods."

After this, Stratonas, recommended to Aristarchus to go to Alexandria, to the Court of Ptolemy II. It is believed that Aristarchus obeyed the recommendations of Stratona and settled in Alexandria which was then an up and coming spiritual center, under the protection of the Ptolemies. There he became director of the famous Library of the Museum of Alexandria, which was an establishment similar to today's Universities.

In Alexandria he remained from 288 until 277 and occupied himself with the study and research of the heavenly bodies.

He wrote many works, but the only one that has survived was his treatise "On the magnitudes and distances of the Sun and the Moon," where, among other things, he determined that the distance of the Sun from the Earth to being 18 or 20 times greater than the distance from of the Moon. Moreover, by means of mathematical calculation, he finds that the size of the Sun is 300 times greater than the size of the earth, and the size of the moon is 30 times smaller than the size of the Earth.

Aristarchus' contribution to Astronomy was tremendous, because it brought it to the highest point that the ancients could reach. Thus, from the above considerations, we can say that Aristarchus' contribution can be divided to two basic areas:

- To the use of instruments and observation.
- To the theoretical interpretation of heavenly bodies.

Worthy of attention and also of some interest is the following: It is said that Aristarchus abandoned his theory, when he couldn't reconcile the hypothetical circular movements of heavenly bodies. Greek astronomers of the day accepted as a given that these orbits were circular. Thus with this activity of his, Aristarchus simultaneously became the Galileo (an Italian mathematician, physicist, and astronomer 1564-1642) and the Copernicus (a Polish monk and astronomer 1473-1543) of the ancient Greek world.

It was an unfortunate thing for the science of the Hellenistic years (the first three centuries B.C.) that the greatest astronomer of the Greeks would attack the heliocentric theory with proofs, in upholding the geo-centric theory which appeared to be indisputable before Copernicus.

Some of his thoughts and views:

- The Sun is the center of the cosmos (Universe).
- The Sun belongs to the class of fixed stars.
- The Sun is the immovable center of the Universe.
- The mass of the Sun is many times greater than the mass of the Earth.
- The Earth revolves around its axis and at an angle around the Sun.
- The Earth in a year revolves around the Sun. The distance of the Sun from the Earth is 18 or 20 times greater than its distance from the Moon.
- The Earth revolves around its axis and in an elliptical circle around the Sun.
- The Earth revolves around the Sun within a period of a year.
- The distance of the Sun from the Earth is 18 or 20 times greater than the Earth's distance from the Moon.

CALLIMACHUS
(310-240 B.C.)

- The oaths that are made in moments of love are kept not even by the gods.
- The honors that were offered me, together with the fragrant and dainty crowns, have immediately died. Of all the pleasant meals my teeth have grounded, nothing was left of them even on the very next day. But, whatever I have heard, these things I always have with me.

THEOCRITUS
(310-245 B.C.)

Theocritus was the chief representative of the Boukolikes muse. He was born at Syracuse of Sicily in 310 B.C., where he also died in 245.

For a long time he lived on the island of Cos, where he attended the lessons of the elegy-writer PHILOTAS and the epigram-writer Asclepiades. He befriended Aratos the poet, to whom he devotes his sixth idyllic, which is considered to be among his greatest poems. After Cos, he lived in his fatherland and at one time in Alexandria, where he was invited in 265 by Ptolemy (King of Egypt) and took on the direction of the famous library.

Around 265 he is found in the court of Ierona (a tyrant of Syracuse) who greatly appreciated the poet.

He spent the last years of his life at the court of the Ptolemies.

THEOCRITUS wrote hymns, funeral songs, elegies, iambs, epigrams and small epics. But his glory is due to *Boukoliki* poetry, which took its name from the *Boukolous* (shepherds of cows) and which he cultivated and extended very much beyond the *boukolous* and shepherds, the farmers and more generally fishermen and men of lower classes from the cities.

From his works it appears that a new power is rising, ROMANTIC LOVE, between man and woman. These noble and immortal feelings of romantic love are different, and are the characteristic features of the Sicilian Theocritus, the last Greek classicisist and the first and greatest of the poets of the Hellenistic epic (the first three centuries B.C.)

Theocritus was a man with vast cultivation and was distinguished as a poet with amazing productivity. It is said that his works fill 800 volumes (cylinders).

His poems were first published by the grammarian (interpreter, text critic) Artemidoros, in about 70 B.C., and his son, Theon, worked on an edition with a commentary.

Theocritus is the only poet of the Alexandrain period who got his inspirations not only from the real world, but primarily from his childhood memories.

The Romans and later the Byzantines admired the poetry of Theocritus very much because of the many human and literary virtues it presented. And thus is explained the great number of writings that were saved on papyra.

Some of his thoughts and views:

- The wisdom of heaven has ordained that the human being needs his or her fellow human beings.
- Only the dead have no hopes.
- The farmer wakes up early and cultivates the ground; the philosopher the soul.
- Blind is not only wealth, but also unthinking, careless love.
- Take courage my friend, tomorrow may be more favorable towards you. As long as life exists, hope also exists. Zeus, who sends storms and rain, likewise also sends a sun-drenched day.
- You must have courage, because perhaps tomorrow it will be better.
- Everyone is in the habit of praising the dead person, while opponents envy the living.
- Necessity is the stimulus of the Fine Arts, and only necessity moves a person to work.
- Wine, my young fellow, can also be called truth.
- The rose is beautiful, and time withers it. The violet too is beautiful in the spring, and it quickly grows old. The flower is all-white, nevertheless, it withers and crumbles up. In like manner, the bloom of youth is beautiful, but it is short-lived.

DEMOPHILUS
(300 B.C.)

Demophilus was an ancient comic poet, who was born, unknown where, in 300 B.C.

He wrote "Onagon," a work that was translated into the Latin language by Marcus, in order for the work to be imitated later by Plautus (a Roman comic and poet 250-184 B.C.) in Aginaria.

Some of his thoughts and views:

- Young people are like plants; from their first fruits we can know what to expect from them in the future.
- The nightingale ordained the beautiful season; and the words of the wise person ordained the peace of the soul.
- Give your trust to people's actions; don't trust their words; no one sees people who, though they live badly, speak good things.
- The mind of the wise, like gold, weighs a lot.

HEROPHILUS
(3rd century B.C.)

Herophilus was the greatest anatomist of antiquity. He was born in Chalcedon (an ancient Greek city of Bosporus), unknown when. In 285 B.C., working in Alexandria, disscected an eye and analyzed the retina and the optic nerves. He divided the brain, described the cerebellum, the temples, gave his name to the so-called veiny region of the Herophilus, and defined the brain as the seat of cognition. He understood the role of nerves; he divided them into sensory and stimulant, and distinguished the nerves of the skull from the nerves of the spinal cord. He made a distinction between arteries and veins, described the function of arteries that transfer blood from the heart to various parts of the body and essentially discovered the circulation of blood 19 centuries before Harvey. He included the taking of pressure in diagnosis, studied the liver and the pancreas and gave the "twelve-finger" the name that it bears until today.

> "Science and art," Herophilus would write, "have nothing to show. Strength is incapable for every endeavor, wealth is useless and eloquence is powerless, when there is no health."

POSEIDIPPUS

(3rd century B.C.)

Poseidippus was a significant poet of comedies from Cassandria, who belonged to attic comedy, which, as it is known, reached its zenith during the 3rd century B.C. He described all the phases of life as follows:

"Which way of life should you prefer? In the market-place there are arguments and pitiful actions. In the homes there are cares. In the fields labor and sweat. In the ocean there are storms. In foreign lands you have no-one: you have fear. If you are poor even marriage is trouble: you cease being without distraction. Children are a pain. Without children, you are drag. What shall one prefer? Not to have been born or to have died the moment one was born?

Let us, however, see a more pleasant perspective.

METRODOROS LAMPSAKINOS

(290 B.C.)

Metrodoros, who was a prominent student of Epicurus (340-270 B.C.), writes:

"You can live happily everywhere. In the market place you see praise-worthy action. In the houses you rest. In the fields are the beauty of nature. In the ocean is profit.

In foreign parts of the world are wonders. Are you married? You'll have an excellent household. Are you unmarried? You'll live without care. The children are a desire. Without children, life is without care.

In youth there is strength. Old age inspire reverence. What should you prefer of the two: Life or death?"

"To be or not to be?" (Shakespeare) Hamlet- Act 3, Scene I .

ARCHIMEDES
(287-212 B.C.)

Archimedes was a wise man of antiquity, a mathematician, a physicist and an engineer. He was born in Syracuse (an ancient Greek city of Sicily) in 287, where he also died in 212 B.C.

Tradition has it that he was a relative or a very close friend of the tyrant of Syracuse Ieronos, to whose son he had dedicated the most significant writing "Psammiti." He was devoted to his particular fatherland, so much, that, even though he had many advantages from remaining in the peaking city of the Alexandria of the Ptolemies at that time, he prefers to live at his birthplace, where he demonstrates his devotion in every way. Thus, as a very small example of his great love towards it, he prefered to use the regional dialect instead of the common Greek language of that time.

During the famous raid of the Syracusians by the Roman Marcellus, he sets in the service of the fatherland all of his great scientific genius.*

In addition to the many real inventions, tradition ascribed other things to him too. Thus, Lucian (an ancient sophist and author 120-200 A.D.) mentions that Archimides, among other things, set the Roman fleet on fire by concentrating on it the rays of the sun with mirrors. This was truly possible and able to be put into effect, but it has not been confirmed historically.

Finally, he sacrifices his very life on behalf of the Syracusians. A certain soldier brutally killed him while he was looking to find new machines, and at that moment, it is said, he said to the soldier who barged into the area he was working, the following famous thing: "Don't upset my formations." Marcellus, who had previously commanded his soldiers to respect the life of the great enemy, was deeply grieved when he heard of his death.

Archimedes, as he himself mentions, was taught astronomy by his father Phedias and had as friend and fellow student Conona (an astronomer from Samos 3rd century B.C.).

He showed great capability and artistry in the manufacturing of machines and especially of astronomical instruments, as well as:

- The study of mirrors led him to the discovery of laws of the Refraction of Light.
- The study of machines led him to the formulation of laws of Mechanics and

* He invented, among other things, machines, for the hurling of large projectiles by means of which his fellow citizens held the Roman raiders afar for a long time.

- There is a tradition that has survived from Bitrubius which states that Archimedes found the laws of hydrostatics by chance while bathing in a tub.

Tradition adds that after the discovery of the law of Hydrostaticism, he ran in the streets naked shouting the immortal "eureka, eureka!"

Archimedes wrote many works that are characterized by originality, completeness, and depth of thought.

It was rightly later said by Leibniz (a German philosopher 1646-1716) that he who understands Archimedes marvels less over the inventions of even the greatest, more modern sages.

From his works the following have survived:

- *On the Sphere and Cylinder*, in which he finds the mass of a sphere and of a cylinder circumscribed within it.
- *On the Circle*, in which he proves the relation ("the logos") of the circumference to the diameter.
- *Psammites,* in which the system of arithmetic of the ancients is described.
- *On Ochoumenon,* in which he develops the well known "Archimedean Principle."

Immortal sayings of his:

- Give me a point on which to stand and I'll move the earth.
- Eureka! Eureka!

CHRYSIPPUS
(280-206 B.C.)

The work of Zeno at the Poikili Stoa was continued by his students Cleanthes and Chrysippus. The latter was the wisest and most productive representative, because he gave the Stoic dogma its historic form, presenting it in 750 books which he wrote. Thus, with Chrysippus, Stoicism spread to all of Greece and Asia. From his massive body of literature fragments have survived by which a synthetic image of the most disseminated Philosophy is displayed, a literature that greatly influenced the ancient world.

Some of his thoughts and views:

- Experience does not necessarily lead to knowledge.
- Everything that our senses relate to us is material and only material things can provoke and accept energy.
- God, like the human being, is living matter. The universe is his body, the order and law of the universe is his intellect and will.

ERATOSTHENES

Eratosthenes was an ancient Greek literary and author who peaked in the 3rd century B.C. He was born in Cyrene (an ancient Greek city of North Africa).

On account of the broadness of his cultivation and the multi-faceted nature of his scientific works, he was considered one of the most important spiritual men of antiquity.

He became director of the famous library of Alexandria. This position of his he maintained until his death.

Eratosthenes occupied himself with the positive sciences (Geography, Mathematics, Astronomy), as well as with the theoretical sciences (Chronometry, Grammatology-a science which studies and critiques the sum-total of the monuments of a Nation.)

He was a pioneer in his scientific studies in Geography, in which, with his trigonometric measurements, set the foundations for the creation of a geographical map and for the comprehension of the region, in all of its special dimensions.

He developed rich and multi-faceted scientific advancements and for this reason was called Philosopher and the New Plato.

His chief work was "Geographics," which he divided into three parts:

- In the first part he examined the History of Geography from the time of Homer till Alexander's successors.
- In the second, which also comprised the most significant part of his writing, he examined Mathematics and Natural Geography.
- In the third he deals with Politics.

For the writing of this important work he traveled to many places and visited many geographers of his time, from whom he learned many things.

Among the works that have survived is also his important mathematical work, which, among other things, referred to the solution of the unsolved problem "concerning the doubling of the cube." His ingenious method became knnown as "Eratosthenes' sifter."

The philosopher also possessed poetic imagination. Astronomy and the starry heaven provided him with the occasion to create the most noteworthy poem, "Hermes," a large part of which has survived.

Eratosthenes suffered from short-sightedness and because he was overcome with fear that he would go blind, he went on a hunger strike and died in Alexandria at the age of 82.

Some of his thoughts and views:

- All the geographers being actuated by a sense of honor made a beginning, but left their work half completed.
- Wine externalizes whatever is hidden in the abyss of the soul.

POLYBIUS
(201-120 B.C.)

Polybius was one of the most remarkable Historiographers of ancient Greece. He is considered the first real historiographer. That is to say, after the description of each serious historical event he sets forth his own judgments and conclusions. This is due to his theoretical cultivation, as well as to his practical knowledge which he acquired from his many trips (for that time) which he took.

He was born in 201 B.C. at Megalopolis of Arcadia, where he also died at the age of 81 (120 B.C.), after an accident (it is said that he fell from a horse).

He was cultivated militarily and politically by Philopoimena (a general of the Achaian Federation 253-183 B.C.).

In the year 181 he was sent, as embassador of the Achaian Federation, to the court of Alexandria (at the end a few words will be said about the city).

In 169 he was chosen head of the Cavalry. Two years later and specifically after the defeat of Persia, he was sent as a hostage, together with other Achaians to Rome, where he became acquainted with a good many Romans. He taught in the home of Aemilius Paul (a Roman general in the 3rd-2nd century B.C.) and accompanied Scipionas Aemilianus (a Roman military officer and politician, who died in 129 B.C.), with whom he became a very close friend, in his great journies to Italy, Galatia and Spain. In 150 he returned to his fatherland, but the following year he returned again to Rome, in order to accompany Scipionas again, now as an engineer, in his third expedition against the Carchedons. Thus was given him the opportunity, being in the Roman fleet, to come to know Northern and Western Africa, and most importantly, to become a witness to the destruction of Carchedon. In the year 133 he was again together with Scipionas, before Numandy, which he destroyed, and later traveled about Spain and again to Galatia. Thus, besides his theoretical education, he also acquired excellent practical knowledge, which allowed him to write a great work "History" consisting of 40 books. In his work he deals with the History of the Romans, the Greeks and the East between the Years 220-146 B.C. Of this history only the first five books have survived completely. From the rest many fragments and summaries survive.

Some of his thoughts and views:

- The study of History can very much contribute to the correction of the life of human beings, because from it we acquire many and wise lessons in life.
- The truth is the most powerful vision, the vision that governs human beings with such imperial supremacy. For even if many fight against it,

and many times the lie is hidden craftily under the appearance of truth, finally it triumphs, defeating every resistance.

- History teaches that egoism is humbled; that the lack of learning, laziness, neglect, carelessness, unmanliness all lead to destruction. On the contrary, diligent application to work, activity, prudence, genius, courageousness, daring, prudence, coolness, steadfastness, are very beneficial and salvific to the life of human beings.

HIPPARCHUS

($1^{st} - 2^{nd}$ Century B.C.)

Hipparchus was considered to be the greatest astronomer of antiquity, the real founder of the science of the heavens, who led Astronomy on the true path. He contributed very much to the progress of Astronomy and more genrally to the "non-philosophical" sciences and is justly considered the true father of Astronomy.

Hipparchus and Aristarchus together constitute the two chief astronomers of antiquity.

He was born in the 2nd century B.C. at Nicea (a historic city of Asia Minor) of Bithynia (a land of Asia Minor). The chronology of his birth and his death, as well as the manner of his death, is unknown.

Of his life very few things are known. The city in which he was born is even doubted, because certain writers have the opinion that he was born in Rhodes. Not even the time of his scientific activity is known.

He was always curious and restless when it came to learning, devoted and endowed with patience in his research and so exact in his observations and announcements, that antiquity called him "Lover of truth."

He occupied himself with almost all branches of astronomy, which he also illuminated and his conclusions held sway for an entire 17 centuries. He performed his studies at Bithynia, at Rhodes and at Alexandria. For these studies, however, he would need instruments and many observations. Thus, he himself produced appropriate instruments which were absolutely indispensable for his heavenly research and observations.

He wrote many works, but only one has survived, namely the one entitled "Of Phenomena." But we know well of him from his treatise Claudius Ptolemy (circa 140 B.C.), who supports his studies on his calculations.

HIS SIGNIFICANT ACHIEVEMENTS:

- He discovered hundreds of stars as well as the use of Trigonometry in Astronomical calculations.
- He was a collaborator in the creation of the first catalogue of constellations and a blackboard depicting eclipses.
- He improved the hypsometer and the quadrants, which were the primary astronomical instruments of his time.
- He invented a method of defining positions on the earth with lines of width and breadth.
- He discovered the relapses of equinoxes (the transposing of Zodiac signs according to ecliptic length.) Thus, human contingencies

conjoined most closely with the constellations and the human soul was considered a part of heaven.

- He created the science of Trigonometry, with the help of elements that had been brought from Babylon.
- He determined, with relative precision, the length of the solar, lunar, and astral year.

He even calculated, approaching great accuracy:

- The ecliptical circle and the orbit of the Moon.
- The highest point of the Sun and the horizontal difference of the Moon.

Equipped with all this knowledge, Hipparchus concluded that the Geocentric view (the theory that the Earth is the center of the Universe) better explains the nature of things than the Heliocentric theory (wherein the Sun is considered the center of the Cosmos-Universe) of Aristarchus, for, the latter, could not withstand mathematical analysis, unless an elliptical orbit of the Earth were supposed.

With these positions of his, Hipparchus reached the point of becoming the greatest theoretician and observer of the ancient astronomers.

Hipparchus followed and studied the heavens continually, when one night he was taken aback by the appearance of a star, of which he was certain had not appeared before. In order to follow its subsequent changes, he wrote, circa 129 B.C., a catalogue, and designed a map and a sphere of heaven in which he marked the positions of 1080 fixed stars, in heavenly length and breadth, something that was a great help for later students of the heavens.

Some of his thoughts and views:

- The Solar year has 365 ¼ days, except for four minutes and 48 seconds (an error of six minutes on the basis of today's calculations).
- The average Lunar month has 29 days, 12 hours, 44 minutes and 2 ½ seconds (a difference of only a second by what is given today).
- The distance of the Moon from the Earth is 250,000 miles (an error of only 5%).
- The Geocentric view better explains the state of things than Aristarchus' hypothesis (i.e., his heliocentric theory-view).

APOLLODOROS

(180-109 B.C.)

- Surely the door closes with bars; however, no architect made a door from which a cat or an adulterer cannot enter.
- Be sorrowful when you see people doing evil; but always believe and expect people's improvement.
- There is no one in the human race with a high stature whom time or envy has not broken.
- Don't desire to be rich or poor; the middle ground is the best. For, if you fall low, financial distress can be covered over. The great mass, however, falling from on high, becomes a big corpse.

DIONYSIUS THE ALICARNASEUS
(1st Century B.C.)

Dionysius was a technographer and historian. He was born in Alicarnassus (an ancient city of Asia Minor near the shore) in the first century. He was taught rhetoric in the Asiatic School and at the age of 25 he went to Rome. There he remained an entire 22 years, learned the Latin language and befriended many prominent Roman senators. He had Rufus Meletius and Ailio Touberona as special protectors. He chiefly occupied himself with the writing of the history of Rome, yet he didn't also neglect Rhetorical instruction which he did as a profession.

The primary historical work of Dionysius is "Roman Archeology") which narrates a history6 of Rome from the beginning until the start of the first Carchedonian war (264 B.C.). There he praises the virtues of the Romans, the purity and strictness of family life, as well as their keen political prudence. He wrote many other works, among which the one full of virtues is entitled "Rhetorical Treatises."

From the surviving works it is proved that Dionysius justly holds first place among critics, because his judgments are ingenious and very exact.

Some of his thoughts and views:

- The love for freedom is innate in all human beings.
- People are accustomed to judging the actions of others according to those actions, which in a similar instance they themselves would have done, and consider things unbelievable from their own perspective.

STRABO
(67 B.C. – 23 A.D.)

Strabo was an author, historian and par excellence the Geographer of antiquity, who was born in 67 B.C. at Amasea (city of Pontus) of rich parents of Greek descent, who secured for himself the means for comfortable studies and an easy life.

His work constitutes one of the most significant sources for the places and peoples of Antiquity known to the Greeks and Romans.

Strabo possessed a full awareness of the practical use of scientific knowledge, as well as a special admiration for Roman politics.

From a young age he studied under great spiritual man, orators and philosophers, resulting in his acquiring a many-sided and multi-faceted education.

In 29 B.C. he went to Rome, where he acquired, not only wise teachers, but also important friends. He studied under the famous philosopher Athenodorus, who had also been the paidagogue of Octavius (a Roman emperor 63 B.C. - 14 A.D.), who also introduced him to Stoic Philosophy, as well as to the theory that the Universe and all the phenomena are pervaded by a unitary principle. Thus, he supported the stoic dogma "Live in accord with nature."

After Rome, Strabo traveled much and visited many lands of the then known world (Greece, Egypt, Syria, Italy, Persia, India, Palestine, Mesopotania, Mediterranean shores, Ethiopia etc.) where he studied the conditions of the regions and the peoples (climate, mores, customs, civilization) and taught and guided various distinguished citizens and rulers.

Strabo was not only a geographer, but also a historian, and his first historical work was *Historical Memoirs,* which contained the history of the known world, from 145 B.C. to the naval battle of Actium (31 B.C.), which, however, has been lost.

His most significant work was *Geographics,* of which only 17 books have survived. It was a product of many years of study, observation, and research. He wrote it during the time of his visit to Egypt and during the last years of his life. In this work, he describes simply and gracefully the lands, peoples and politicians he encountered and relies upon Eratosthenes and on other Greek historians and geographers.

Strabo considered Geography (and he persisted in this view) to possess a political character. That's why the greater part of the *Geographics* refers to nations and rulers, though collectively he is concerned with the occupations of the people in power. At any rate, from the very first lines he sets forth the view that Geography constitutes Science.

It is clear that the greater part of the *Geographics* is supported by foreign sources, though personal experiences appear interspersed here and there, even though Strabo himself mentions that he had visited many countries. Nevertheless, he was very careful in his choice of information. At all events, the Geography of Strabo is something very much more than simple Geography; it resembles more an encyclopedic book of knowledge, relating to the countries of the known world during the beginning of the period after Christ. In the last analysis it's about Historical Geography, or according to certain students, it's about the philosophy of geography.

Strabo died about 23 A.D., unknown where, but as in the case of his date of birth, so also his time of death has not been exactly determined. It is only a probable conjecture.

Some of his thoughts and views:

- Live according to nature.
- The Romans imitated the Greeks completely aimlessly.
- The Earth is a sphere, like the world and is found at the center of the Universe.
- Religion is necessary and the basis of morality.
- All events and all actions of the will are determined.
- It is impossible for something to happen differently from the way it is happening.
- The human being is to the Universe what the mirocosm is to the macrocosm.

EPICTETUS
(50-120 B.C.)

Epictetus was a stoic philosopher who was born in Ierapolis of Phrygia (an ancient city of Asia Minor) about 50 A.D. and died in Nicopolis of Epirus in 120 A.D..

He was a contemporary of Nero and Traianus, and was the slave of Epaphroditus. He initially lived as a slave in Rome, where he heard the lessons of the stoic philosopher Mousonius.

His calmness and stoicism was proverbial. It is said that though his master, in order to test his dispassionateness, cut the flesh of his rear shin with a sharp instrument, Epictetus turned towards him and said dispassionately: "You'll break it," and when he broke the bone, the philospher said: "I told you beforehand." From then on it is said that he remained crippled, though it is more probable that he was cripple from birth.

After the purchasing of his freedom, he became a teacher of Philosophy in Rome, from where he was expelled, together with other philosophers, circa 90 A.D., after an ordinance that Domitianus made (a Roman emperor 51-96 A.D.), against the philosophers, in general, because he had feared their liberal spirit of instruction. He drew away to Nicopolis of Epirus (it was built in the 1st century B.C. by the Roman emperor Octavius Augustus 63 B.C.- 14 A.D., after his victory in the naval battle of Actium; it peaked in the 6th century and its decline must have occurred in stages after the 8th century and was completed in the 11th century) and there he gathered his students, who had come together from Rome and continued his instruction, being greatly admired for his simplicity, and strict and great frugality (he lived in Rome under a roof, without using furniture, except for a table and a hay cot that he used for sleep. In Nicopolis he lived even more frugally).

The basis of his teaching, which bears clear traces of Seneca's (a Roman author and philosopher 2-66 A.D.) influence, was his Ethics and practical sermons of a religious character.

According to Epictetus:

- The principle of happiness consists of knowledge of what depends and what does not depend on our will.
- Love towards people is a duty, since we are all children of the one God.

Epictetus was one of the most faithful interpreters of pure stoicism, because his teaching was absolved of every petty theory and was limited to moral rules that regulated the practical behavior of people in their daily lives. He constitutes, together with Seneca and Marcus Aurelius, (a Roman emperor and philosopher, famous for his virtue and goodness, 121-180 A.D., who would say: "Consider human matters always as being transient, without value. Pass the moment, which is called life, in all its duration according to nature and reach the end calmly.") the most prominent representatives of the more modern period of stoic philosophy.

His rich philosophical and didactic work was written down by his student Arrian in eight books, the "Diatribes," of which only half survive in the form of a synoptical "handbook," called the Enchiridion, which has survived completely undamaged.

Some of his thoughts and views:

- Love for people is a duty because we are all children of the one God.
- Self-sufficiency is a quick and delightful path, which, though providing great pleasure, gives little annoyance.
- Laziness is the root of evils, while diligence is the mother of every virtue.
- Happiness is to acquire goods and to enjoy them, but not to desire them.
- We must not fear poverty, nor exile, nor jailing; we should fear itself.
- It is more necessary to cure our soul than our body, because death is preferable to a bad life.
- We all tremble at spiritual (intellectual) paralysis and we try in every possible way to avoid it. Yet, no one cares about psychical paralysis, or paralysis of the soul.
- Educate your children. It is better to leave them behind educated than wealthy. For they will be able to hope for better things with an education than with wealth.
- Things don't disturb people, only the opinions that they form about things. Death is not something fearful. If it were, it would have appeared so to Socrates.
- Don't wish for things to be as you like, but wish for things to be as they are, and then you'll be happy.
- How can one enjoy the same things, who does not knock on the doors of the powerful, as one who does knock on them? The one who doesn't become their follower and one who does? The one who praises them and the one who does not?
- Determine for yourself a character, a way of life and maintain it without change, either when you are alone or when you meet with others.
- When someone tells you that you don't know anything and you don't take offense and are not bothered by it, then know that you are beginning to implement Philosophy.

- Whoever knows how to subject himself or herself to need is wise, and possesses knowledge of the gods.
- The most just laws are the most true.
- It is better for you to die of hunger and have neither sorrows nor fears, than to live with abundant goods together with cares and unrest.
- If you want your children and your wife and your friends to live eternally, you are being foolish. That is to say, you want to exercise power over those things that don't lie within your power. Also, foreign things don't belong to you.
- Remember that the one who insults and strikes does not offend; only the idea behind these things is offensive.

PLUTARCH
(46-127 A.D.)

Plutarch was the most important of the ancient Greek Prose writers, who was born in 46 A.D. at Cheroneia of Boetia, where he also died in 127.

He studied Philosophy at Athens. He traveled to Alexandria and Rome, where he remained a long time and became associated with the Court of Traianus (Roman emperor 42-117 A.D.), and later became a teacher of the emperor Adrian (1st – 2nd century A.D.)

When he returned to Greece, he acquired the offices of ruler and priest of the Pythian Apollo.

His life was developed in a very small circle of friends, but he was a symbol for the power of the Greek spirit, which focused on the great past, without, however, also neglecting the demands of the present.

Plutarch was not only a historical researcher and well known Biographer, but also an Encyclopedist and Philosopher. Of all the things that he wrote, in his various studies and monographs, it is clear that he was a great admirer and follower of Platonic Philosophy. He could not also, however, escape from the influence of other Schools and especially the Peripatetic School of Aristotle.

Plutarch gave special attention to the problem of Ethics and to the issue of Religion.

This was only natural, since, in his time, the various intellectuals would hone their judgment and thought on these issues, because their time was seeking a new response to them. For this reason is most prolific Historical researcher and religious Philosopher attempts, by studying Stoicism and, even more, Platonism, to give solutions to the philosophical Problems of his time. Yet, as greatly cultivated encyclopedically and well read is he was, his was not a creative mind. That's also the reason why he had no new philosophical system to present.

We must mention that Plutarch was an exponent of Orphism, of Pythagorianism, as well as of the Eastern Priestly Wisdom. For this reason, he places great significance on religious and priestly traditions.

According to his philosophy, the universe is a creation of divine energy and he imagined this energy to be Providence.

He wrote about 85 works, the most important of which are;

- *Parallel Lives*, in which are presented biographies of famous Greeks and Romans, written in a charming and didactic style. They are valuable for the historical elements that they offer.
- *Ethics,* which include different treatises relating to elements of various Sciences, Philosophy, Archeology, Sociology, Politics, History, Natural Sciences, etc.

Some of his thoughts and views:

- Knowledge is for the spirit whatever the eyes are to the body, that is, light. On the contrary, ignorance and lack of learning are darkness.
- Happiness is not an accurate scale for friends. The only scale on which to weigh friends is misfortune.
- Philosophy is the art of life.
- The soul closes within it the power of love, because just as it was formed to feel, to think, and to remember, thus too it was created to love.
- Just as we must prepare for winter in the summer, so too we must in our youth acquire orderliness and prudence, which are valuable equipment for old age.
- Diligence and instruction and labor to a great degree supplement the voids of nature.
- Glory increases after death, because then envy ceases.
- Paideia, education, is an element of happiness, not only for the home, the city, the state but for the whole human race.
- There is no wilder beast than the human being, when he or she possesses a power that is equal to his or her passion.
- The worst animal among the wild ones is the tyrant, and among the peaceful ones, the flatterer.
- The first principle of conquering is to be courageous.
- Health is a divine and pleasant dessert.
- Prudent people draw lessons from their own mistakes.
- Those who falsely praise someone who has no value blind and lead him or her to perdition.
- Just as the clouds darken the sun, so do the passions darken reason.
- The virtuous and wise person has no need for glory.
- The magnanimous person, the steadfast person, shines even in disasters and during misfortunes with all of his or her brilliance.
- The most acceptable prayer to God is the one that comes from a heart full of good disposition and gratitude.
- Many were destroyed because because they believed in those things that they should not have believed, and on the contrary, did not believe in those things that they should have believed in.
- Perhaps falling into error is not a mark of the wise person. Nevertheless it is human.
- Power and authority reveal each fault of a person.
- We should not be overly happy in our good times, nor full of sadness in bad times. Niether should we be dissolute in our pleasures, nor in our anger unconstrained and monstrous.
- Never ridicule a person who has fallen in misfortune.

Printed in Great Britain
by Amazon

67945500R00121